The Supported Learning in Physics Project
has received major support from

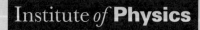

The project is also supported by
The Department for Education and
Employment

PHYSICS, JAZZ & POP

This unit was written by
Richard Skelding and Mike Bethel

THE SUPPORTED LEARNING IN PHYSICS PROJECT

Management Group

Elizabeth Whitelegg, Project Director, The Open University

Professor Dick West, National Power Professor of Science Education, The Open University

Christopher Edwards, Project Coordinator, The Open University

Professor Mike Westbrook, Vice-President for Education, Industry and Public Affairs, The Institute of Physics

George Davies, Manager, College Recruitment, Ford of Britain

Geoff Abraham, Project Trailing Manager

Dorrie Giles, Schools Liaison Manager, Institution of Electrical Engineers

Martin Tims, Manager, Education Programme, Esso UK

Catherine Wilson, Education Manager (Schools and Colleges), Institute of Physics

Production

This unit was written for the Project by Richard Skelding, East Norfolk College, and Mike Bethel, Penrhos College, Clywd.

Other members of the production team for this unit were:

Elizabeth Whitelegg, Project Director

Christopher Edwards, Project Coordinator

Andrew Coleman, Editor

John Coleman, Course Assessor

Alison George, Illustrator

Keith Hodgkinson, Unit Assessor

Julie Lynch, Project Secretary

Sian Lewis, Designer

Cartoons supplied by ABC Cartoons

The authors and Director wish to thank David Tawney and Ken Dobson for their helpful comments and advice whilst writing this unit, and the staff of the International Convention Centre, Birmingham, for their cooperation in the production of this unit.

ISBN 0 435 68838 3

The Institute of Physics, 76 Portland Place, London, W1N 4AA.

First published 1996 by Heinemann Educational Publishers.

© 1996 The Institute of Physics.

Printed in Great Britain by Bath Press Colourbooks, Glasgow

For further information on the Supported Learning in Physics Project contact the Information and Marketing Officer, The Centre for Science Education, The Open University, Walton Hall, Milton Keynes, MK7 6AA.

1.1

	HOW TO USE THIS UNIT	5
1	INTRODUCTION	7
2	SOUND	9
	Ready to Study test	9
2.1	Wave graphs	11
2.2	Music and noise	12
2.3	Loudness, wavelength and frequency	14
2.4	How are frequency and wavelength connected?	16
	Achievements	21
	Glossary	21
	Answers to questions	22
3	VIBRATIONS AND SOUND	23
	Ready to Study test	23
3.1	Free vibrations	24
3.2	Natural frequency of vibration	26
3.3	Forcing and damping vibrations	29
3.4	Wave terminology	33
	Achievements	37
	Glossary	37
	Answers to questions	38
4	SOUNDS FROM MUSICAL INSTRUMENTS	41
	Ready to Study test	41
4.1	Stringed instruments	42
4.2	Vibration of strings	46
4.3	Patterns of string vibrations	48
4.4	Wind instruments	51
4.5	Pipe frequencies	57
4.6	Patterns of pipe resonances	63
4.7	Pipe end corrections	64
	Achievements	68
	Glossary	68
	Answers to questions	69
5	PROPAGATION VELOCITY	72
	Ready to Study test	72
5.1	Velocity of a wave in a string	74
5.2	Velocity of a sound wave in air	75
5.3	Velocity of sound in a solid	78
	Achievements	80
	Glossary	80
	Answers to questions	80

CONTENTS

6	WAVES MEETING OBSTACLES AND OTHER WAVES	84
	Ready to Study test	84
6.1	Diffraction	85
6.2	Interference	87
6.3	Beats	89
	Achievements	91
	Glossary	91
	Answers to questions	91
7	RECORDING AND REPRODUCTION OF A CONCERT	94
8	TRANSDUCERS	95
	Ready to Study test	95
8.1	Microphones	96
8.2	Loudspeakers	100
	Achievements	106
	Glossary	106
	Answers to questions	106
9	AMPLIFICATION	109
	Ready to Study test	109
9.1	The functions of amplifiers	110
9.2	Characteristics of a 'black box' amplifier	112
9.3	Amplifiers and human hearing	117
	Achievements	120
	Glossary	120
	Answers to questions	122
10	STORAGE MEDIA	124
	Ready to Study test	124
10.1	Magnetic tape	124
10.2	Compact discs	127
	Achievements	132
	Glossary	132
	Answers to questions	133
11	RECORDING AND REPRODUCTION SYSTEMS	135
11.1	Recording a concert	135
11.2	Reproduction of music in a disco	135
12	ACOUSTICS OF A LARGE HALL	136
12.1	Introduction	136
12.2	Inside the Symphony Hall	138
12.3	Quantifying the acoustics of a hall	140
	Achievements	143
	Glossary	143
13	CONCLUSION	144
	ACKNOWLEDGEMENTS	145
	INDEX	146

This unit introduces you to a new method of studying – one that you probably won't have used before. It will provide you with a way of studying on your own, or sometimes in small groups with other students in your class. Your teacher will be available to guide you in your use of this unit – giving you advice and help when they are needed and monitoring your progress – but mainly you will learn about this topic through your own study of this unit and the practical work associated with it.

We expect that you will study the unit during your normal physics lessons and also at other times – during free periods and homework sessions. Your teacher will give you guidance on how much time you need to spend on it. Your study will involve you in a variety of activities – you won't find yourself just reading the text, you will have to do some practical work (which we have called 'Explorations') and answer questions in the text as you go along. (Advice on how long each exploration is likely to take is given.) It is very important that you do answer the questions as you go along, rather than leaving them until you reach the end of a section (or indeed the end of the unit!), as they are there to help you to check whether you have understood the preceding text. If you find that you can't answer a question, then you should go over the relevant bit of text again. Some questions are followed immediately by their answers but you should resist the temptation to read the answer before you have thought about the question. If you find this difficult it may be a good idea to cover up the answer with a piece of paper while you think about the question. Other slightly longer or more demanding questions have their answers at the back of the section. Most sections also have a few difficult questions at the end. You are likely to need help with these; this might be from a teacher or from working with other students.

Most sections start with a short 'Ready to Study' test. You should do this before reading any further to check that you have all the necessary knowledge to start the section. The answers for this test are also at the end of the section. If you have any difficulties with these questions, you should look back through your old GCSE notes to see if they can help you or discuss your difficulties with your teacher, who may decide to go over certain areas with you before you start the section or recommend a textbook that will help you.

The large number of practical explorations in the unit are designed to let you thoroughly immerse yourself in the topic and involve yourself in some real science. It is only after hands-on experiences that you really begin to think about and understand a situation. We suggest that you do some of these explorations with other students who are studying the unit and, when appropriate, present your results to the rest of the class. Because there are such a large number of these explorations it would be impossible for you to do all of them, so if everyone shares their results with others in the class you will all find out about some of the explorations that you are unable to do. At the end of the unit there is a project that we hope everyone will be able to do.

Your teacher will arrange times when the practical work can be undertaken. For health and safety reasons you must be properly supervised during laboratory sessions and your teacher will be responsible for running these sessions in accordance with your school's or college's normal health and safety procedures.

Other activities may involve you in some research using your school facilities or local libraries. You may wish to collaborate with others for these sorts of activities and to pool your efforts. Being responsible for your own learning does not mean that you always have to work alone. Working in pairs or groups can help your learning, and using this unit in a variety of ways will help you to develop your skill as an independent learner.

HEALTH AND SAFETY NOTE

The unit warns you about any potential hazards and suggests precautions whenever risk assessments are required of an employer under the Management of Health and Safety at Work Regulations 1992. We expect that employers will accept these precautions as forming the basis for risk assessments and as equivalent to those they normally advocate for school science. If teachers or technicians have any doubts, they should consult their employers.

However, in providing these warnings and suggestions, we make the assumption that practical work is conducted in a properly equipped and maintained laboratory and that field work takes account of any LEA or school or college guidelines on safe conduct. We also assume that care is taken with normal laboratory operations, such as heating and handling heavy objects, and that good laboratory practice is observed at all times.

Any mains-operated equipment should be properly maintained and the output from signal generators, amplifiers, etc., should not exceed 25 V rms. For the explorations that use the strobe light, strobe frequencies below 20 Hz should be avoided.

A jazz band in full swing

It can be an exciting and stimulating experience to go to a live concert in a good concert hall. You will appreciate the skills of individual performers, especially if you play a musical instrument yourself, but you may ask yourself 'Why do they sound so much better than I do at home and how are they able to produce such sounds on their instruments?'

If you can't be at the concert you may buy a tape or a CD – how do they work? What is the difference between a good hi-fi system and a bad one?

These questions involve a lot of physics; this unit will introduce you to all the concepts you need to answer them. Here is a summary of the physics topics you will meet in this unit:

- work, power and efficiency
- potential and kinetic energy
- conservation of energy
- electric current, potential difference and resistance
- electric circuits
- material properties
- simple harmonic motion
- free and forced vibrations
- resonance
- damping
- wave types and properties
- diffraction and superposition of waves
- stationary waves
- kinetic theory
- magnetic fields
- magnetic force on a current
- electromagnetic induction.

In addition to this, you will get plenty of practice using physics apparatus, some of which you possibly haven't used before – oscilloscopes, for example.

Even if you're not an amateur instrumentalist, you will no doubt have 'entertained' your teachers at some time to an unrehearsed concert by twanging rubber bands, flicking a ruler held over the edge of a table, blowing over a pen top or using pencils as drumsticks.

To get the feel of this unit, we suggest that you carry out the following exploration in small groups of 2–4 for each of the sets of equipment.

'Enthusiastic sound production'

E Exploration 1.1

30 MINUTES

There are seven sets of sound-producing equipment available:

1 A rubber band and a board with some nails fixed in it, between which the band can be stretched at different tensions

2 Several rulers

3 Three milk bottles and a jug of water

4 Three pen tops or test-tubes of different lengths

5 Three metal rods to suspend by cotton from stands

6 Stretched strings on an old guitar or violin

7 A tin whistle or recorder

You will also need some metre rules.

Try to decide how you are going to investigate each set of sound-producing equipment in your small groups. You should devise an organized strategy to find the factors that control the loudness and the pitch (how 'high' or 'low' the note is) of each set.

We suggest you get used to making a formal record of all your experimental work. Your record of this exploration could be organized as follows:

■ name of the set of sound producers

■ description of the ways in which the loudness can be changed

■ description of the ways in which the pitch can be changed.

When you have finished investigating all seven sets, discuss with the other groups any factors affecting the way in which sound is produced and controlled that are common to several sets.

One common property you should have found is that all the sources vibrated.

The context for studying the physics topics listed on page 7 is music – how it is made, recorded, reproduced, enhanced by a good concert hall, etc. But music is sound, so we will approach things more generally for the time being.

You will already have some appreciation of what sound is and that it involves energy being transferred from one place to another by sound waves. In this section you will learn how to represent sound waves graphically and you will investigate some of the characteristics of sound (and waves in general). This will involve using electronic equipment, deriving mathematical relationships and carrying out calculations.

READY TO STUDY TEST

Before you begin this section you should be able to:

■ draw and interpret graphs

■ interpret traces of waveforms on an oscilloscope (measurement of amplitude and period)

■ draw and interpret simple block diagrams representing experimental set-ups.

You should also be able to explain:

■ the relationship between velocity, displacement and time (time taken = displacement/velocity)

■ the relationship between velocity, frequency and wavelength (velocity = frequency × wavelength)

■ the relationship between the frequency of a wave and its periodic time (frequency = 1/time period).

QUESTIONS

R1 A stationary dolphin emits a pulse of sound through the sea under water. A second stationary dolphin is 2000 m away. How long does it take the sound to travel through the water from the first dolphin to the second dolphin? (Velocity of sound in sea water at 20 °C is 1522.2 m s^{-1}.)

R2 A trumpeter plays a note with a frequency of 523 Hz. If the velocity of sound in air at 20 °C is 343 m s^{-1}, how many complete wavelengths will fit between the trumpet and the ears of a listener 66.0 m away?

SOUND

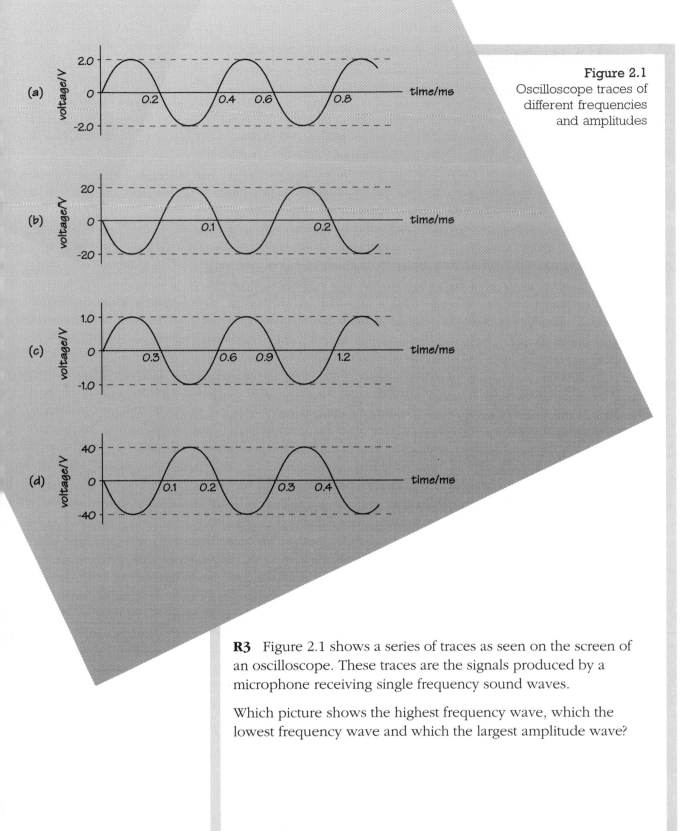

Figure 2.1
Oscilloscope traces of different frequencies and amplitudes

R3 Figure 2.1 shows a series of traces as seen on the screen of an oscilloscope. These traces are the signals produced by a microphone receiving single frequency sound waves.

Which picture shows the highest frequency wave, which the lowest frequency wave and which the largest amplitude wave?

2.1 Wave graphs

Human beings observe how their surroundings are changing in many ways. Two of the most important are by reference to time passing and by reference to distances from a fixed place (usually the spot where the person is).

You can also look at waves in the same way, as shown in Figure 2.2.

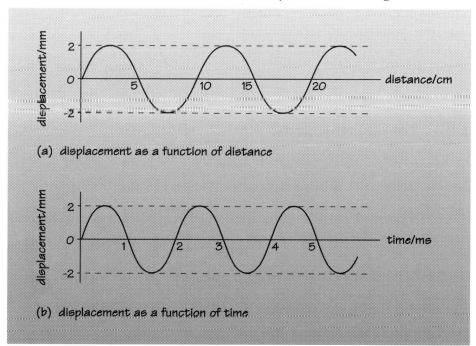

(a) displacement as a function of distance

(b) displacement as a function of time

Figure 2.2
Particle displacement as a function of distance and time

Sound is the movement of the particles of the medium that is carrying it, e.g. the molecules of air if the sound is travelling through air. From Figure 2.2(a) you can measure or calculate the **wavelength** as well as the **displacement** of the particles of the medium that is carrying the wave. The particles vibrate, i.e. they move backwards and forwards without actually 'flowing' – the sound moves through the medium leaving the medium in its original position after it has passed. The maximum particle displacement is the **amplitude** of the particle vibration. From Figure 2.2(b) you can obtain the time period of the particle oscillation. From the time period you can calculate the **frequency**.

 What is the amplitude of the particle vibration in Figure 2.2?

2 mm.

 What is the frequency of the particle vibration, and therefore of the sound?

The time period, T, of the vibration is 2 ms, so the frequency, f (the number of vibrations per unit time), is $1/T$, which is 0.5 vibrations per millisecond or 500 vibrations per second. So the frequency is 500 Hz.

2.2 Music and noise

From your experience of the world you could categorize the sounds you hear as broadly falling into two main types: **musical sounds** and non-musical sounds (of which most can be classified as **noise**).

Sometimes the difference between music and noise depends on personal opinion, which can change with a person's age – your parents may disagree with your definition of music! Scientific methods, however, can show you what the differences are and help you to decide which is which, as the following experiment shows.

20 MINUTES

E Exploration 2.1 Looking at sounds

Apparatus:

◆ loudspeaker ◆ signal generator ◆ oscilloscope
◆ microphone ◆ amplifier

Set up the apparatus as shown in Figure 2.3(a). Adjust the **signal generator** output to give a sound from the **loudspeaker** that is comfortable to hear. Choose a frequency in the range 200–1000 Hz, use the sine wave output if you have the choice. Adjust the Y-input sensitivity control on the **oscilloscope** to give a wave crest to wave trough height of half the screen. Adjust the timebase control so that three or four complete wave cycles (corresponding to three or four complete time periods) are clearly seen.

If you are unable to obtain a stable picture ask your teacher to help.

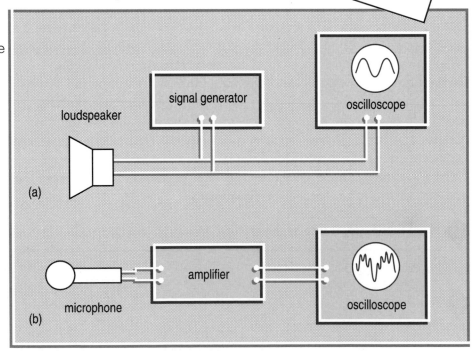

(a)

(b)

Figure 2.3 Arrangement of apparatus for Exploration 2: (a) loudspeaker connection, (b) microphone connection

Do the sounds you are hearing have a musical quality? You should be able to see the electrical picture of the sound wave on the screen and note that it has a repeated regular shape. The length (converted into a time using the timebase setting) of one of the repeating shapes or cycles (a whole crest and a whole trough) is one time period.

Switch off the signal generator and then disconnect it from both the oscilloscope and the loudspeaker and connect the **microphone** (via an amplifier) to the Y-input of the oscilloscope, as shown in Figure 2.3(b). Now sing or whistle a note of fixed **pitch** and **loudness** into the microphone to give a similar sized set of waves to those you obtained with the signal generator. It is easier if a partner sings or whistles while you adjust the oscilloscope controls to get a stable picture. If anyone in your group plays an instrument they could try to play the note that has just been sung or whistled into the microphone.

If the experiment has worked so far, you should have been able to see stable waveforms; they would have looked something like those shown in Figure 2.4.

Now make some noise into the microphone. This can be done in many ways, remembering that the oscilloscope controls (Y-input sensitivity and timebase control) may need adjusting to produce a clearly observable picture on the screen as you produce the noise. Make the following noises:

Noise 1   A tin of small nails randomly shaken.

Noise 2   A saucepan with a few marbles rolling about at the bottom.

 Draw the waveforms you observed on the oscilloscope screen.

Describe the main difference between the noise waveforms and the musical note waveforms. How do the noise waveforms change if you make the noises more energetically?

Can you find a typical time period to associate with these noises?

You would have noticed that there was no apparent regularity in the noise waveforms, but there was in the musical note waveform. The amplitude of the noise waveform increases as you put more energy into making the noise. A random waveform with no measurable time period is characteristic of noise. In contrast, musical notes have measurable time periods corresponding to regular waveforms.

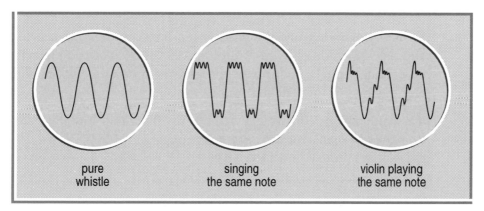

Figure 2.4   Oscilloscope waveforms of musical sounds

2.3 Loudness, wavelength and frequency

You will have noticed in the experiments that you have done so far that to produce a louder sound you had to put more energy into the sound source. You can check how this affects the shape of the sound wave produced by repeating the first part of Exploration 2.1 and varying the energy output of the signal generator.

 Exploration 2.2

Apparatus:

◆ loudspeaker ◆ signal generator ◆ oscilloscope

Choose a frequency on the signal generator of about 500 Hz and adjust the oscilloscope controls to give an amplitude (height of a crest or half the vertical distance between the bottom of a trough and the top of a crest) of about 2 cm. Now change the size of the signal generator output to make the sound louder. Observe how the size and shape changes on the screen. Then, just to confirm your observations, change the loudness level to very quiet (you may now need to adjust the sync control on the oscilloscope to stabilize the trace).

> There is a risk of damaging equipment by handling connectors and wires incorrectly when making connections to the signal generator, loudspeaker, etc. Follow the points below when undertaking this exploration.
> 1 Make sure all the equipment is switched off whilst setting up the circuit.
> 2 All connectors and the loudspeaker terminals must be insulated. Do not use bare connectors such as 'spade' connectors or crocodile clips.
> 3 Switch off before making any physical adjustments to the circuit.

15 MINUTES

? Arrange the traces shown in Figure 2.5 into order of increasing loudness for the sounds that produce them. Read the scales on the displacement and time axes carefully before you write your list.

The order you have should be: (b), (a), (c).

So now you understand the relationship between the loudness of a sound and the amplitude of its associated wave. The next sound property to investigate is pitch – what wave property is associated with making a high-pitched or low-pitched sound?

It is worth noting at this point that the terms 'pitch' and 'loudness' are more from the musician's vocabulary than the physicist's. Physicists would measure 'frequency' and '**intensity**'.

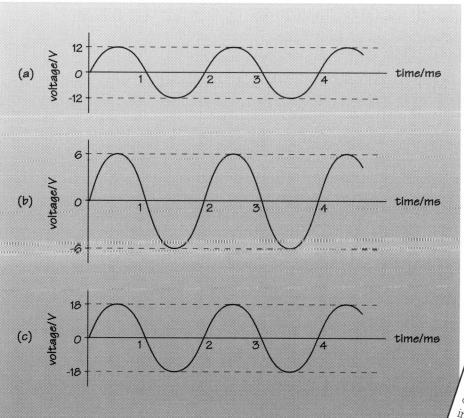

Figure 2.5
Oscilloscope traces
of signals from a
microphone
detecting sound
waves of differing
loudness

 Exploration 2.3

Apparatus:

◆ loudspeaker ◆ signal generator ◆ oscilloscope

Adjust the signal generator output to obtain a trace on the
oscilloscope that almost fills the screen from top to bottom
and then set the signal generator frequency to 150 Hz,
adjusting the oscilloscope timebase control so that you
see one to two waves on the screen. Next, while
simultaneously watching and listening, change the signal
generator frequency in steps of about 200 Hz up to about 950 Hz.

There is a risk of damaging
equipment by handling
connectors and wires
incorrectly when making
connections to the signal
generator, loudspeaker, etc.
Follow the points below when
undertaking this exploration.
1   Make sure all the equipment
is switched off whilst setting up
the circuit.
2   All connectors and the
loudspeaker terminals must be
insulated. Do not use bare
connectors such as 'spade'
connectors or crocodile clips.
3   Switch off before making
any physical adjustments to
the circuit.

15
MINUTES

(i) What happened to the pitch of the sound and its associated wave as you
increased the frequency?

(ii) Arrange the waveforms in Figure 2.6 overleaf in order of increasing frequency.
(Take careful note of the time scales shown.)

(iii) Complete the following sentence by filling in the gaps with appropriate words.
A quiet, high-pitched sound has a _____ amplitude, a _____ frequency and a _____
period than a loud, low-pitched sound.

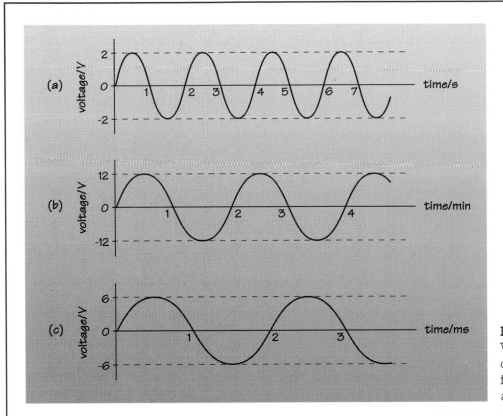

Figure 2.6
Waveforms of differing frequency and amplitude

(i)   The pitch rose and the time period (and associated wavelength) became shorter.

(ii)   The lowest frequency has the longest time period, therefore the order of increasing frequency is (b), (a), (c).

(iii) Appropriate words are 'smaller' (or 'shorter'), 'larger' (or 'longer'), 'smaller' (or 'shorter').

2.4 How are frequency and wavelength connected?

As you know, frequency and wavelength *are* connected. If the frequency of a wave is increased, the wavelength decreases. How does this happen?

Q1 If the velocity, v, of a water wave is 0.10 m s^{-1} and the frequency, f, at which waves are produced is 3.0 waves every second, what is the wavelength, λ? What is the wavelength if 6 waves are produced every second? ◆

Q2 The end of a stretched slinky spring is oscillated at 1 Hz. Waves 0.25 m long are observed to travel down the spring. Calculate the velocity of the waves in the slinky. ◆

To see why there is this inverse connection you need to think of a much more obvious type of wave than a sound wave: water waves for example – at least you can see these and watch them moving about.

E Exploration 2.4 Measurements on water waves

Ask for advice from the PE Department for normal precautions to observe when working by swimming pools or ponds.

45
MINUTES

Apparatus:

◆ three metre rules ◆ three stopwatches ◆ long-handled sweeping brush

Ideally a group of you (6–12) need to find a large expanse of water where you can control the surface behaviour more or less as you wish. You could use a local swimming pool out of normal swimming hours by prior arrangement with its manager, or a fishpond in a friend's garden if the weather is calm. However, just one or two people can do the same experiment on a smaller scale using a plastic tray several centimetres deep half-filled with water. You can also do it at home in the bath! Modify the equipment you use according to the scale of your experiment.

The experimenters need to divide the tasks (making the waves, following the wave crests and measuring the wavelength) between them.

The wave makers. Oscillate the brush in a vertical mode, with the head just in the top 10 cm of the water surface, to produce a series of fairly regular waves (with an amplitude of about

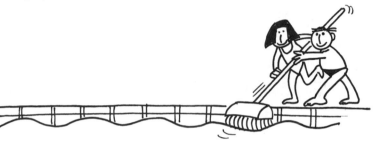

10 cm) that can be identified by members of the other two teams. You will need to practise the oscillating until you can produce a constant wave frequency. You could try several frequencies in the range 2 Hz to 0.5 Hz. (This means the wave crests should follow each other with time intervals of between 0.5 s and 2 s.)

The wave crest observers. Time how long a particular wave crest takes to travel a fixed distance along the water surface and do lots of repeated measurements to get a reliable value for the average speed of travel of the water waves.

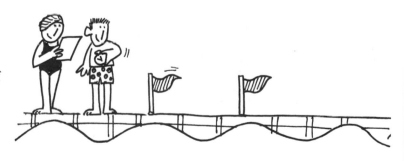

The wavelength measurers. This is the trickiest job as you have to measure the distance (along the direction of travel) between adjacent crests as they move across the surface. You will need to do plenty of repeated measurements at each frequency of brush oscillation in order to get a good average value for each wavelength. When you've finished the experiment produce a summary table like the one shown overleaf.

wave frequency (Hz)	wavelength (m)	wave speed (ms⁻¹)

If you now look at each row of values (making some allowance for imperfections in your measurements) you should be able to spot a simple algebraic relationship between the three measured quantities.

You should find that:

$$v = f \times \lambda$$

where

v = wave speed

f = wave frequency

λ = wavelength

You don't need to do an experiment to derive the relationship $v = f\lambda$ if you consider the following story.

In Figure 2.7 the wave is travelling with a velocity v and has a wavelength λ. If any point in the wave moves past the fixed post and continues for 1 s, then it will have moved a distance v past the post. The number of wavelengths that will occupy this distance will be given by v/λ. In other words v/λ waves will pass a fixed point in 1 s – this is the definition of the frequency of a wave, i.e.

$$\frac{v}{\lambda} = f$$

which rearranges to

$$v = f \times \lambda$$

which is what you should have found from the exploration.

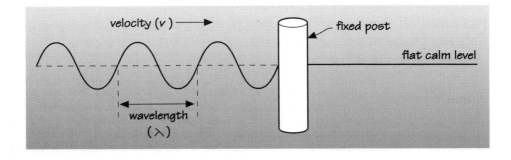

Figure 2.7
Waveform for water waves travelling across a pond

ⓔ Exploration 2.5 The speed of sound in air

Apparatus:

◆ signal generator ◆ dual trace oscilloscope
◆ microphone ◆ loudspeaker

In this exploration you will measure the wavelength of a
sound wave and use its value and the frequency to calculate
the speed of sound using the relationship:

$$v = f \times \lambda$$

You need to set up the apparatus as it is shown in
Figure 2.8. The oscilloscope must be set to 'dual trace'.
Set the signal generator frequency to 1000 Hz, the wave shape to sine
and the amplitude to low. Switch it on and adjust the amplitude until the
loudspeaker produces a reasonably loud sound. The oscilloscope will then be able to
give you two traces; one is the signal coming directly from the signal generator, the
other is the signal from the microphone. The two traces should be similar, the microphone's
signal is the result of the electrical signal from the signal generator being converted into
sound by the loudspeaker and then back into an electrical signal by the microphone.

30 MINUTES

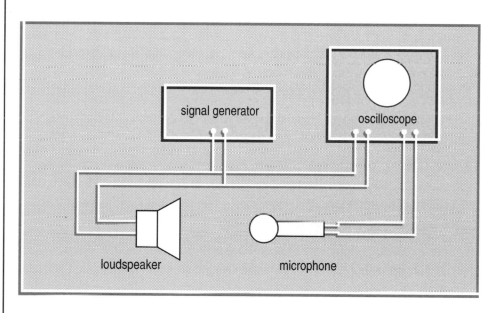

Figure 2.8

Move the microphone towards and away from the loudspeaker. If you ignore the
changing amplitude of the signal from the microphone (the sound is obviously louder
nearer to the loudspeaker) you will see the **phase** relationship between the two signals
changing. The horizontal axis for the two oscilloscope traces is time, so the signals have
the same form but what they are doing at a particular time can be different.

When the two signals match exactly they are said to be 'in phase'; when they are doing
exactly the opposite they are in 'anti-phase'. In between these two extremes they are
'out of phase' to some extent. You can express the extent to which two signals are out of

19

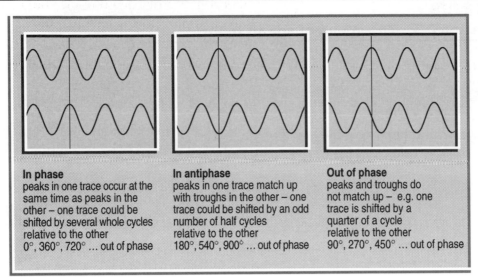

In phase
peaks in one trace occur at the same time as peaks in the other – one trace could be shifted by several whole cycles relative to the other
0°, 360°, 720° ... out of phase

In antiphase
peaks in one trace match up with troughs in the other – one trace could be shifted by an odd number of half cycles relative to the other
180°, 540°, 900° ... out of phase

Out of phase
peaks and troughs do not match up – e.g. one trace is shifted by a quarter of a cycle relative to the other
90°, 270°, 450° ... out of phase

Figure 2.9

phase as a fraction of a cycle or in degrees – 360° being a complete cycle. If two signals are 360° out of phase they are so far out of phase that they are in phase again! See Figure 2.9.

The phase relationship changes because, as you move the microphone, the distance the sound has to travel from the loudspeaker to the microphone changes. The further it has to travel, the greater the delay between the arrivals at the oscilloscope of the signal that travelled via the loudspeaker and microphone and the electrical signal travelling by the constant, higher-speed route through the direct wire link.

The distance travelled by a wave in one cycle is the wavelength, so if you move the microphone away from the loudspeaker by a distance equal to one wavelength you will add a phase difference of one cycle, or 360°.

Find a position at which the two signals are in phase and then move the microphone further away from the loudspeaker until the two signals are in phase again. Measure the distance you moved the microphone and you now know the wavelength. Repeat this several times and get an average value for the wavelength.

Use your value for the wavelength (in metres) and the frequency set on the signal generator (1000 Hz) to calculate the speed of sound in air (in m s^{-1}).

Achievements

After working through this section you should be able to:

- use the musical terms 'loudness' and 'pitch' and relate these to the physics terms 'amplitude' and 'frequency'

- differentiate between musical sounds and noise

- describe how energy is used to produce sounds

- draw graphs of displacement against time and displacement against distance for waves and interpret these graphs

- state the difference between a high- and a low-energy sound wave and know how to show this graphically

- apply the wave equation that connects wave velocity to its frequency and wavelength

- explain the meaning of phase and express it in terms of a fraction of a cycle of a wave and in degrees

- use the following apparatus safely: signal generators, oscilloscopes, loudspeakers and microphones

- explain the advantages in practical work of preplanning, group organization, practice runs, repeat measurements and thorough record keeping in building up your experimental efficiency

Glossary

Amplitude   Maximum displacement.

Displacement   The distance moved by a particle from its rest position or from the centre of its vibrating path.

Frequency   The number of complete vibrations in a given time interval.

Intensity (I)   Unit: watt per metre squared, $W\,m^{-2}$. This term is often applied to sound; it is the sound power passing through unit area perpendicular to the direction of propagation of the sound. It can be applied to any energy transfer process.

Loudness   The subjective effect of sound intensities on the ear and brain.

Loudspeaker   A device for converting varying electric currents into mechanical vibrations, and thus into pressure waves (sound).

Microphone   A device for converting sound waves in air into mechanical vibrations and then into varying electric currents.

Musical sounds   Sounds that are generally considered to be pleasant. Their associated waves have regular periodicity and a detectable wavelength.

Noise   Sounds that are generally considered to be unpleasant. They have no detectable wavelength or regular periodicity in their associated waveforms.

Oscilloscope   A piece of equipment to produce a visual display of one or more electrical signals; generally it includes a cathode-ray tube similar to a television set.

Phase   The horizontal position-matching of two electrical signals as observed on the screen of an oscilloscope. Two time varying signals that keep 'in step', so they reach maximum positive voltage at the same time, and so on, are said to be 'in phase'. Phase difference is measured in degrees, so 'in phase' can mean the phase difference is 0° or any multiple of 360°. If two signals are 180° (or 540° etc.) 'out of phase' then they are mirror images of one another.

Pitch   The musical term describing whether a note sounds 'high' or 'low', i.e. whether it has a high or low frequency.

Signal generator   A piece of electronic apparatus that can produce alternating currents at varying amplitudes and frequencies.

Wavelength   The distance between two adjacent wave crests or between two adjacent wave troughs.

Answers to Ready to Study test

R1

$$\text{Time taken} = \frac{\text{distance}}{\text{velocity}}$$

so

$$\text{time taken} = \frac{2000}{1522.2\,\text{m s}^{-1}}$$

$$= 1314\,\text{s}$$

R2

$$\text{Wavelength} = \frac{\text{velocity}}{\text{frequency}}$$

so

$$\text{wavelength} = \frac{343\,\text{m s}^{-1}}{523\,\text{s}^{-1}}$$

$$= 0.656\,\text{m}$$

so number of waves fitting into the distance

$$= \frac{66\,\text{m}}{0.66\,\text{m}}$$

$$= 100$$

R3

Wave (b) has the highest frequency since its time period of 0.10 ms (the curve crosses the time axis exactly on 0.1, so we can write 0.10) is the shortest of the four waves.

Time period is the time it takes the wave to execute a single cycle and the frequency in Hertz is the number of waves in 1 s, therefore

$$\text{frequency in Hz of wave (b)} = \frac{1}{\text{time period}}$$

$$= \frac{1}{0.10\,\text{ms}}$$

$$= \frac{1}{0.10 \times 10^{-3}\,\text{s}}$$

$$= 1.0 \times 10^4\,\text{Hz}$$

Wave (c) has the lowest frequency as it has the longest time period of 0.60 ms (the curve crosses the time axis exactly on 0.6, so we can write 0.60). Therefore

$$\text{frequency of wave (c)} = \frac{1}{0.60\,\text{ms}}$$

$$= \frac{1}{0.60 \times 10^{-3}\,\text{s}^{-1}}$$

$$= 1.7 \times 10^3\,\text{Hz}$$

Wave (d) has the largest amplitude – the amplitude of a wave is measured from the zero displacement level (0 V on Figure 1d) to the maximum height (or depth) of the wave (40 V on Figure 1d).

Answers to questions in the text

Q1

$$v = 0.10\,\text{ms}^{-1}$$
$$f = 3.0\,\text{Hz}$$

Since

$$\lambda = \frac{v}{f}$$

$$\lambda = \frac{0.10\,\text{m s}^{-1}}{3.0\,\text{s}^{-1}}$$

$$= 0.33 \times 10^{-1}\,\text{m}$$

$$= 3.3 \times 10^{-2}\,\text{m}$$

When

$$f = 6.0\,\text{Hz}$$

$$\lambda = \frac{v}{f}$$

$$= 1.7 \times 10^{-2}\,\text{m}$$

Q2

$$f = 1.0\,\text{Hz}$$
$$\lambda = 0.25\,\text{m}$$

Since

$$v = f\lambda$$

$$v = 1.0\,\text{s}^{-1} \times 0.25\,\text{m}$$

$$= 0.25\,\text{ms}^{-1}$$

Sound is caused by mechanical vibrations; in many musical instruments these vibrations are set up in strings or air columns.

In this section you will begin to investigate how devices produce sounds of particular frequencies; this leads naturally into the ways in which musical instruments work.

READY TO STUDY TEST

Before you begin this section you should be able to:

- describe the period or periodic time of an oscillation
- explain how a spring behaves in terms of the force it exerts for a given extension, in particular, with reference to the relationship $F = -kx$, where F is the force, k is the spring constant and x is the extension of the spring
- explain the meaning of potential energy and kinetic energy
- use the expression for kinetic energy, $E = \frac{1}{2}mv^2$, where m is the mass of the moving body and v is its velocity.

QUESTIONS

R1 A pendulum swings from one extreme of its motion to the other (say from left to right) in 1.0 s. What is the periodic time, T, of its oscillations?

R2 A spring is 10 cm long when no force is acting upon it. It is 12 cm long when it is stretched by a force, F, of 4.0 N. What force needs to be used to stretch it to 20 cm?

R3 A ball with a mass, m, of 2.0 kg is dropped from the top of a building that is 20 m high. How fast is the ball travelling when it hits the ground? (Take g to be 10 m s^{-2} and neglect air resistance.)

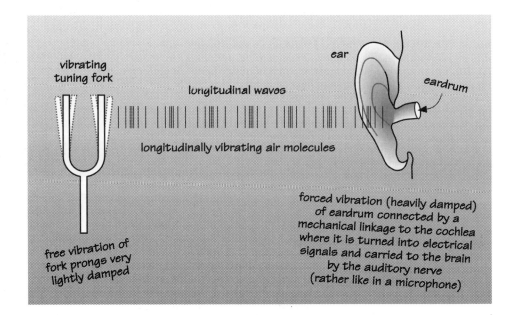

Figure 3.1
Transmission of sound

Figure 3.1 shows examples of different types of vibration as the **tuning fork** vibrates and the sound produced travels to the ear and makes the eardrum vibrate in turn. The prongs of the tuning fork vibrate at a constant frequency after energy is supplied by hitting it. As the prongs move from side to side they change the air pressure – these pressure changes affect the air around the tuning fork and a pressure wave (sound with the same frequency as the frequency of vibration of the tuning fork prongs) moves away from the tuning fork. Eventually these changes in pressure reach the eardrum. A pressure lower than the normal atmospheric pressure in the inner-ear will cause the eardrum to move out and a higher pressure than normal will move it inwards. So the eardrum ends up vibrating at the same frequency as the frequency of the tuning fork. Your auditory nerves detect this vibration and send a signal to your brain to give you the sensation of hearing. This is a complex situation which needs to be broken down into small steps.

3.1   Free vibrations

The tuning fork, used in the example above, was undergoing **free vibration**. After being hit initially it continued to vibrate. There was nothing external to the tuning fork itself that controlled its frequency of vibration. You might wonder why it vibrates at a particular frequency – it clearly has its own particular natural frequency. There are, of course, lots of other examples.

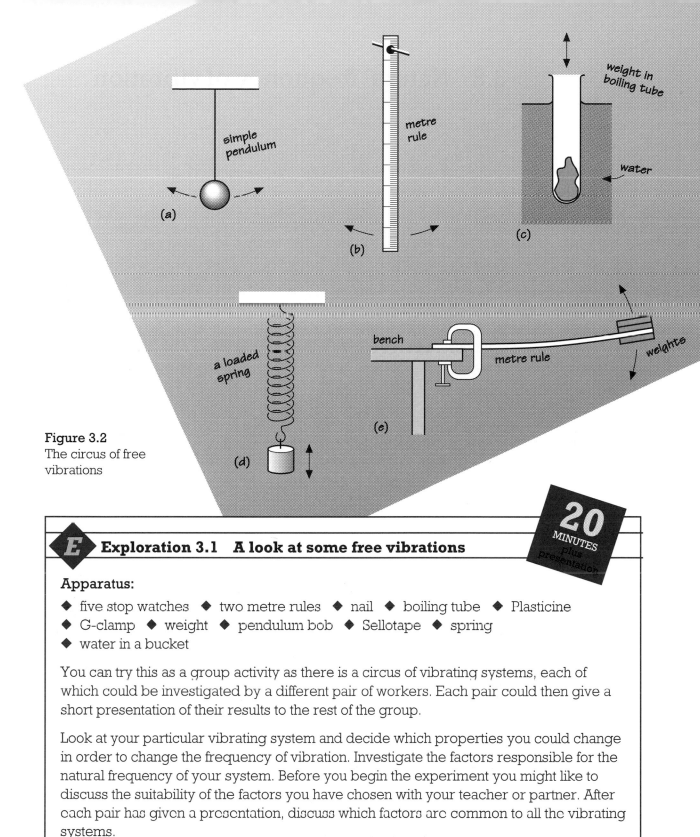

Figure 3.2
The circus of free vibrations

E Exploration 3.1 A look at some free vibrations

Apparatus:

◆ five stop watches ◆ two metre rules ◆ nail ◆ boiling tube ◆ Plasticine
◆ G-clamp ◆ weight ◆ pendulum bob ◆ Sellotape ◆ spring
◆ water in a bucket

You can try this as a group activity as there is a circus of vibrating systems, each of which could be investigated by a different pair of workers. Each pair could then give a short presentation of their results to the rest of the group.

Look at your particular vibrating system and decide which properties you could change in order to change the frequency of vibration. Investigate the factors responsible for the natural frequency of your system. Before you begin the experiment you might like to discuss the suitability of the factors you have chosen with your teacher or partner. After each pair has given a presentation, discuss which factors are common to all the vibrating systems.

The amplitude of vibration can easily be maintained by applying small, occasional forces that are in step with the vibration – just as you keep a child's swing moving.

3.2 Natural frequency of vibration

To understand why a system has a natural frequency at which it will vibrate, you can consider a simplified system (as in Figure 3.3). It has the important features common to all the examples you have investigated and to the tuning fork and all musical instruments.

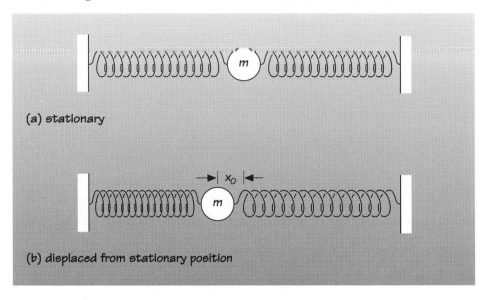

(a) stationary

(b) displaced from stationary position

Figure 3.3
A simplified vibrating system

The mass, m, is held in position by two identical springs. Initially it is at rest with the two springs applying equal forces to it: it is at its **equilibrium position**. It can be set into vibration by displacing it from this position by an amount x_0 and releasing it. The vibration will gradually get less until it is at rest at its equilibrium position again; this is due to damping by friction, energy losses in the springs and air resistance. All the examples in Exploration 3.1 involved a moving mass and opposing forces, so our simplified vibrating system has the same important features.

Now, imagine there is no damping. Once the vibration has started it will go on for ever.

The force exerted by a spring (assuming it has not been stretched or compressed too much) is proportional to the amount by which it has been stretched or compressed:

$$F \propto x$$

or

$$F = -kx$$

where k is a constant for the particular spring (known as the **spring constant**).

The minus sign indicates that the force acts in the opposite direction to the direction in which the spring has been distorted. When the mass is moved to the left, as in Figure 3.3, the force on it will be to the right and proportional to the displacement from the equilibrium position. Once it is released the force moves m towards its equilibrium position, elastic potential energy is converted into kinetic energy. The force is zero when *m* reaches the equilibrium position, but it has gained a lot of kinetic energy, so it passes through this position. The direction of the force now changes. *m* is moving to the right but the force is acting to the left, so *m* slows down. Kinetic energy is converted into elastic potential energy. When all the kinetic energy has been converted, *m* has moved as far to the right as it was to the left at the start. The same sequence of changes occurs, but the other way round.

So, the force trying to *restore m* to its equilibrium position is given by:

$$F = -kx$$

as $F = ma$ and therefore $a = F/m$, the acceleration of *m* at any position *x* is

$$a = -\left(\frac{k}{m}\right)x$$

The velocity is determined by the acceleration; as *a* has a particular value at every value of *x* the same will apply to the velocity, *v*. As *v* has specific values at each position it is clear that the journey of *m* from left to right and back again (one complete vibration) always takes the same time, so the periodic time of vibration is fixed. Therefore the frequency of vibration – the *natural frequency* – has a particular value. As *a* depends upon *k* and *m*, the frequency, *f*, will also depend upon the springs (or other means of supplying the restoring force) and the mass of the vibrating object.

 A freely oscillating body with a mass of 0.1 kg has a velocity of 0.2 m s^{-1} when it passes through its equilibrium position. What will be the increase in the potential energy of the system when the mass has moved to its maximum displacement position?

The mass has maximum kinetic energy as it passes its equilibrium position, this will be given by:

$$E = {}^1\!/_2 mv^2$$
$$= 0.5 \times 0.1 \times (0.2)^2 \text{ J}$$
$$= 2.0 \times 10^{-3} \text{ J}$$

All this energy is converted into potential energy by the time the mass reaches its maximum displacement position – at this point its velocity is zero. So the increase in the potential energy of the system is equal to the decrease in the kinetic energy, i.e. 2.0×10^{-3} J.

The preceding analysis describes **simple harmonic motion**. This is expressed by the equations:

$$x = x_0 \cos(2\pi f t) \tag{3.1}$$

$$v = -2\pi f x_0 \sin(2\pi f t) \tag{3.2}$$

$$a = -(2\pi f)^2 x_0 \cos(2\pi f t) \tag{3.3}$$

where t is the time from the release of m from its original displaced position, x_0. (See Figure 3.4.)

(Simple harmonic motion is described here only briefly. A more complete description can be found in another unit in the series – *Physics for Sport*.)

Some syllabuses use $x = x_0 \sin(2\pi f t)$ and this changes the equations for v and a, but does not change $a = -(2\pi f)^2 x$.

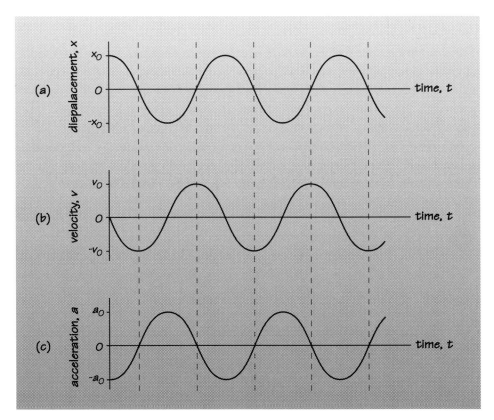

Figure 3.4
Displacement, velocity and acceleration as a function of time for a body with simple harmonic motion

By combining Equations (3.1) and (3.3), we get

$$a = -(2\pi f)^2 x \tag{3.4}$$

(or $a \propto -x$)

Comparing this with

$$a = -\left(\frac{k}{m}\right)x$$

results in

$$f = \frac{1}{2\pi}\sqrt{\frac{k}{m}}$$

An analysis of any vibrating system can, therefore, result in an equation for the system's natural frequency.

The relationship

$$a \propto -x$$

must apply to the system for its vibration to have truly simple harmonic motion. If the restoring force is not proportional to the displacement, or there is damping, the equations above will not be true for the system. However, although they do not exactly apply to some of the systems in Exploration 3.1, they are often good approximations for some of the time while the system is freely vibrating.

Q1 The approximate expression for the natural frequency of oscillation of a pendulum is:

$$f = \frac{1}{2\pi} \sqrt{\frac{g}{l}}$$

where g is the acceleration of free fall ($10\,\mathrm{m\,s^{-2}}$) and l is the length of the pendulum.

What is the length of a pendulum with a period of oscillation of 1.0s? ◆

3.3 Forcing and damping vibrations

Forced vibrations

You may also have experienced these on a swing at an early age. If you called 'faster, faster!' the 'energy injector' may have replied that they couldn't push you faster, they could only push you higher. When you were older you may have tried to make a swing go faster yourself, but with little success. You would have found that it was possible to make a swing vibrate at a frequency dictated by you only if there was a very small person on the swing, you were very strong, had a very tight grip and kept hold of it all the time you were applying the driving force. You would be able to manage this for a very short time only, as it is very exhausting. It takes a lot of energy input to keep a **forced vibration** going.

A forced vibration of any system occurs when the system is connected to an external driver. The driving system needs to be tightly and continuously attached to the driven system. The amplitude of the forced vibrations can be maintained only by the application of large amounts of energy from the driver. Good examples of forced vibrations are shown by the cone of a loudspeaker and your eardrum, which are 'designed' for the job. It is most difficult to force systems to vibrate at frequencies other than their natural ones if they are highly tuned and have very little damping.

Exploration 3.2 Barton's pendulums – an example of free (resonant) and forced vibrations

20 MINUTES

Apparatus:

◆ 200 g mass   ◆ five small identical weights   ◆ thread   ◆ two tall stands

See Figure 3.5 for details of how the array of pendulums should look. The large mass driver needs to be made of lead or brass and have a smooth surface to reduce air resistance. The smaller pendulums could be identical small brass weights

For this exploration to work well, it is essential that the length of the central driven pendulum (pendulum C in Figure 3.5) is identical to the length of the driver, while the lengths of the others should be systematically longer or shorter, as shown in Figure 3.5.

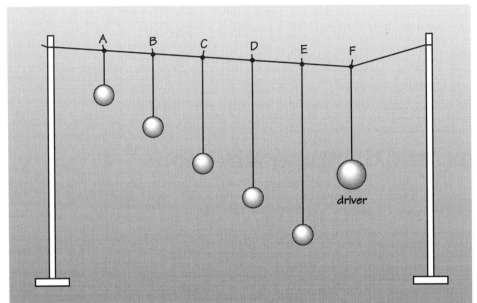

Figure 3.5 Barton's pendulums

 By discussion with your partners, or by very careful experimentation, decide on which of the three lengths in the simple pendulum shown in Figure 3.6 accurately determines the time period of its vibration.

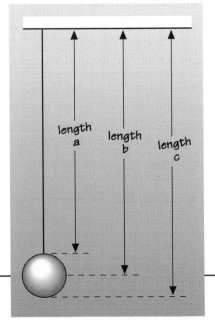

Figure 3.6 What is the critical length for a pendulum?

The critical length is from the point of suspension to the centre of gravity of the bob – length b.

Pull back the driver pendulum and let it go so that it will execute vibrations at right angles to the plane containing all the pendulums. Carefully observe what happens. You may need to repeat the experiment several times in order to check your observations. Do not dismantle your experiment yet.

Using your observations and your knowledge of free and forced vibrations, write an explanation of your results.

Q2 By referring to the observations you made while carrying out the last exploration answer the following questions.

(a) What is the source of the energy gained by the light pendula?

(b) What is the important feature of the light pendulum that gained most energy in the exploration?

(c) Was the oscillation of the light pendulum that gained most energy in step with that of the heavy pendulum?

(d) Did the other light pendula oscillate at the same frequency and in step with the heavy pendulum? ◆

Damped vibrations

All real vibrating systems have vibrational amplitudes that decrease with time unless energy is put into them continuously.

 Think up some reasons why this may be so.

All vibrators make contact with other atoms or molecules as they vibrate, such as surrounding fluids or a framework that the vibrator is connected to. As the vibrator moves it will force the surrounding molecules to move. This movement of the surroundings takes energy from the vibrator. Energy will be taken away faster if the mass of surrounding molecules forced into vibration is large rather than small, so the vibrator will keep vibrating for a shorter time. This loss of energy by a vibrating system is called damping, and the vibrations in such a system are called **damped vibrations**.

Exploration 3.3   Damping Barton's pendulums

Apparatus:

◆ 200 g mass ◆ five small identical weights ◆ thread ◆ two tall stands ◆ paper

Make some small paper cones which can be slipped over the small weights used in Exploration 3.2. Repeat the exploration.

Q3 What main differences did you observe between using the weights on their own and increasing the air resistance by adding the light cones? Discuss these differences with your partners and try to explain why they occurred. ◆

The degree of damping of a vibrating system can be described in two main ways, as in Figure 3.7.

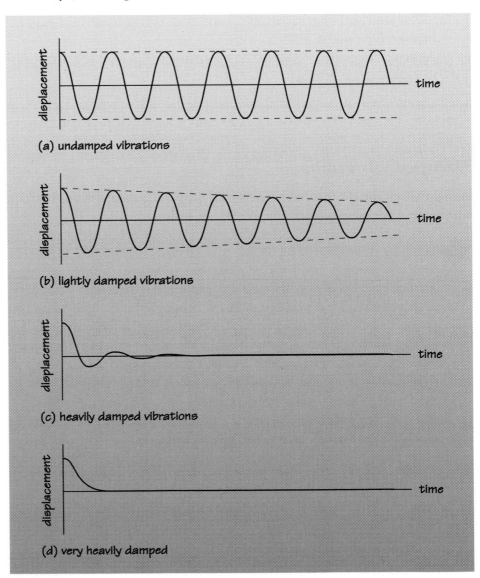

Figure 3.7
Degrees of damping

Q4 Think about some common vibrating systems and decide, in discussion with your partners, whether they require a particular type of damping to allow them to behave as they should. You could consider various moving toys, civil engineering structures and musical instruments. ◆

3.4 Wave terminology

You may have already come across the terms **longitudinal** and **transverse** applied to waves. They describe ways in which the particles of the medium carrying a wave vibrate. There are many more terms that describe wave motion, as this next paragraph illustrates. It describes how energy is transferred from an instrument to your ear.

A guitar string executes resonant or free vibrations to produce a **stationary**, transverse wave on the string. This forces the air between the source (the guitar) and your ear to carry a **travelling**, longitudinal wave. The eardrum is then forced to vibrate and this enables you to hear sounds. (Its vibrations are heavily damped, so they are not sustained.)

Longitudinal waves

The direction of vibration of the particles in the medium carrying the wave is in the same direction as the direction of travel of the wave energy (see Figure 3.8a). Sound waves are a good example of longitudinal waves. As sound is carried by a medium, such as a gas, the particles of the medium alternately move closer together (producing a **compression** at higher than normal pressure) and further apart (a **rarefaction** at lower than normal pressure).

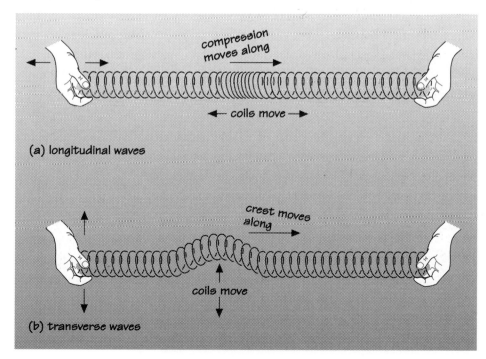

(a) longitudinal waves

(b) transverse waves

Figure 3.8
Longitudinal and transverse waves

Transverse waves

The direction of vibration of the particles in the medium carrying the wave is at right angles (transverse) to the direction of travel of the wave energy (see Figure 3.8b). Water and string waves are good examples of transverse waves.

You may be interested to know that an earthquake produces both transverse and longitudinal waves simultaneously in the surrounding rocks.

Travelling waves

The positions of maximum and minimum particle displacement move through the medium at the velocity of the wave that is being carried (see Figure 3.9a). Ripples on water are a good example of this.

Stationary waves

Here the opposite occurs. The positions of the maximum and minimum amplitude vibration are fixed (see Figure 3.9b). If you watch one point along the wave the only change in the vibration amplitude you would see would be a 'damping down' due to the vibrating medium losing energy to its surroundings. Vibrating strings and air columns are good examples.

A stationary wave is the combination of two travelling waves of equal amplitude and wavelength but travelling in opposite directions (with opposite velocities). In the case of columns of air, the wave can be reflected from the closed end of the enclosing pipe. In the case of strings, reflection occurs at the fixed ends. The reflected wave travels in the opposite direction to the original wave.

Figure 3.9
Travelling and stationary waves

The sound frequencies produced by stationary waves in musical instruments are dependent on the vibrational properties of the particles of the medium carrying the wave – in the case of a string it is the string's length, tension and mass per unit length.

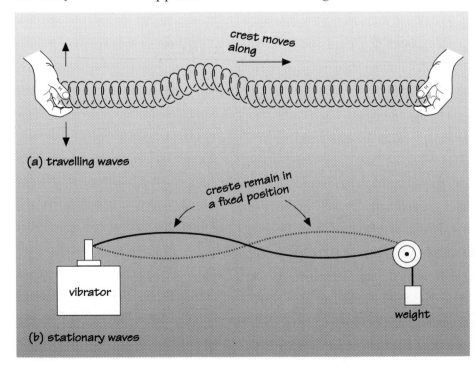

crest moves along

(a) travelling waves

crests remain in a fixed position

vibrator

weight

(b) stationary waves

Exploration 3.4
Travelling waves causing a stationary wave on a string

Apparatus:

- ◆ signal generator ◆ audio vibrator ◆ thin string or thread
- ◆ small weights (20 g, 10 g) ◆ small pulley ◆ strobe light

Set up the apparatus as shown in Figure 3.10.

You need to work in subdued lighting so that the string is illuminated predominantly by strobe lighting. Adjust the strobe frequency so that it is almost the same as the string frequency.

Experiment with the string tension so that at a vibrator frequency of about 50–100 Hz you can produce a stationary wave with three loops in it as suggested by Figure 3.10. (The point where the string is attached to the vibrator cannot be a node, because the string must move, but if the amplitude of the vibrations of the vibrator are small this point is close to the node, which will actually be beyond the end of the string.) Adjust the signal generator to give the largest possible amplitude. When the strobe frequency is close to the signal generator frequency you will be able to see a wave travelling up and down the string and being reflected at each end.

Q5 What did you notice about the wave just after it had been reflected from one end? It may be helpful to try Exploration 3.5 before coming to a final answer. ◆

20 MINUTES

All participants and observers should wear safety spectacles or goggles for this exploration. Any stretched material may cause serious eye injury if it snaps.
Put a cardboard carton on the floor under the weights to keep your feet out of the way in case the wires break.
Strobe lights can cause epileptic fits in some people. Do not look directly into the flashing strobe light – view the string from the side of it. Do not turn the frequency of the strobe light below 20 Hz.

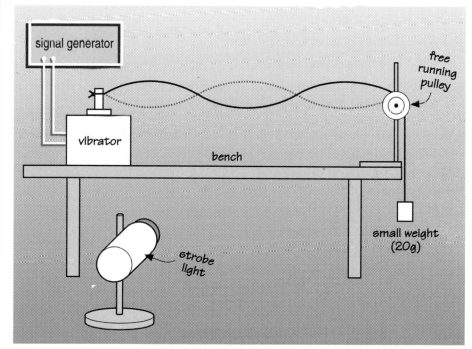

Figure 3.10
The arrangement for Exploration 3.4

E **Exploration 3.5   Reflecting a slinky wave pulse**

Apparatus: ◆ slinky

10 **MINUTES**

You need an assistant on the floor with you. Make a single, sideways (transverse) flick of your end of the slinky, making sure your partner holds the other end very firmly. Observe what happens to the pulse amplitude just after reflection. Repeat if necessary.

The following questions are quite demanding, you are likely to need some help to answer them fully, accurately and efficiently. Ask a teacher for assistance or work with other students.

Q6 (a) A pendulum bob is pulled to one side and released. Viewed from below, the bob has simple harmonic motion. What provides the horizontal force on the pendulum bob?

Take the horizontal restoring force, F, on the bob to be $(mg/l)x$, where m is the mass of the bob, g is the acceleration of free fall, l is the length of the pendulum and x is the horizontal displacement.

(b) What is the acceleration, a, as a function of x?

(c) Use Equation (3.4) given earlier to determine expressions for the pendulum's natural frequency, f, and periodic time, T. ◆

Q7 The amplitude of oscillation of a body with simple harmonic motion is 1.0 m, its displacement 1.0 s after being released from its maximum displacement position is 0.50 m.

(a) What is its frequency of oscillation?

(b) What is its velocity at 1.0 s?

(c) How long from the moment of release does it take to pass through its equilibrium position for the first time? ◆

Q8 A car has spring suspension. When the car is loaded and the driver gets in (a total load of 200 kg) the suspension is compressed by 30 mm. The total mass of the car and load is 1000 kg. What is the natural frequency of oscillation of the car now? ◆

Achievements

After working through this section you should be able to:

- explain the difference between free and forced vibrations

- produce an argument to explain why freely vibrating systems have a natural frequency

- identify the features of a simple harmonic oscillator

- describe simple harmonic motion

- draw graphs of the displacement, velocity and acceleration of a body with simple harmonic motion

- use the terms 'potential energy' and 'kinetic energy' in describing the behaviour of an oscillator

- describe an experiment to demonstrate the transfer of energy by forced vibration

- explain the difference between compression and rarefaction of fluid particles along the path of a sound wave and say how they are caused

- explain the difference between travelling and stationary waves and between transverse and longitudinal waves

- relate the degree of damping of a vibrating system to its rate of vibrational energy loss.

- use the equation $F = -kx$.

Glossary

Compression   A region of higher than average density due to the squeezing together of the material particles as the sound wave passes through.

Damped vibrations   Vibrations whose amplitude decreases with time; damping can be light or heavy.

Equilibrium position   The position at which the total force on a mass is zero.

Forced vibrations   Vibrations produced in a system by external forces acting on that system and controlling its frequency.

Free (resonant) vibrations   Vibrations of a system when no external forces control its frequency.

Longitudinal wave   A wave where the direction of vibration of the particles carrying the wave is the same as the direction in which the wave is travelling.

Rarefaction   A region of lower than average density caused by the stretching apart of the material particles as a sound wave passes through.

Simple harmonic motion   Oscillatory motion in which the acceleration (or force acting) is always towards the equilibrium position (position of zero net force), and its magnitude is proportional to the displacement of the oscillating body from this position. This is defined by the equation $F = -kx$, where k is the constant for a particular spring, F is the restoring force and x is displacement from the equilibrium position.

Spring constant   The constant, k, equal to the ratio of the force, F, exerted by the spring and the amount, x, by which it has been stretched or compressed, so $F = -kx$.

Stationary or standing wave   The pattern of particle vibration amplitude caused when a string or wind instrument is played. There are fixed positions along the string or air column where the particles have maximum or minimum vibration displacements.

Transverse wave   A wave where the direction of vibration of the particles carrying the wave is perpendicular to the direction in which the wave travels.

Travelling wave   The pattern of particle vibration amplitude when a sound passes through a medium. The positions of maximum and minimum particle displacements move through the medium at the velocity of the sound in that medium.

Tuning fork A simple musical 'instrument' with steel prongs that can vibrate at a precise frequency determined by the manufacturer. Commonly used as a reference when tuning musical instruments.

Answers to Ready to Study test

R1

One complete oscillation would bring it back to its starting point, i.e. back to the left again, so the periodic time is twice the time for the motion described, i.e.

$T = 2 \times 1.0\,\mathrm{s}$

$\quad = 2.0\,\mathrm{s}$

R2

$x = 12\,\mathrm{cm} - 10\,\mathrm{cm}$

$\quad = 2.0\,\mathrm{cm}$

$F = -kx$

so

$k = \dfrac{F}{-x}$

$\quad = \dfrac{-4.0\,\mathrm{N}}{-2.0\,\mathrm{cm}}$

$\quad = 2.0\,\mathrm{N\,cm^{-1}}$

When the spring is 20 cm long

$x = 20\,\mathrm{cm} - 10\,\mathrm{cm}$

$\quad = 10\,\mathrm{cm}$

$F = -kx$

$\quad = -2.0\,\mathrm{N\,cm^{-1}} \times 10\,\mathrm{cm}$

$\quad = -20\,\mathrm{N}$

so a force of 20 N must be applied.

R3

The ball has more gravitational potential energy when it is at the top of the building, this will be converted into kinetic energy as it falls, increasing its velocity.

Decrease in potential energy = increase in kinetic energy

As the ball had no kinetic energy initially this can be restated as:

Final kinetic energy = decrease in potential energy

i.e.

$\frac{1}{2}mv^2 = mg\,(\text{change in height})$

$\qquad\quad = mg\,(\text{height of building})$

$\qquad\quad = mgh$

so

$v^2 = 2gh$

$v = \sqrt{2gh}$

$\quad = \sqrt{2 \times 10\,\mathrm{m\,s^{-2}} \times 20\,\mathrm{m}}$

$\quad = \sqrt{400\,\mathrm{m^2\,s^{-2}}}$

$\quad = 20\,\mathrm{m\,s^{-1}}$

Answers to questions in the text

Q1

Rearranging the equation to make l the subject produces:

$l = \dfrac{g}{(2\pi f)^2}$

$f = \dfrac{1}{T}$

$\quad = \dfrac{1}{1.0\,\mathrm{s}}$

$\quad = 1.0\,\mathrm{Hz}$

so

$$l = \frac{10\,\mathrm{ms}^{-2}}{(2\pi \times 1.0\,\mathrm{Hz})^2}$$

$$= 0.253\,\mathrm{m}$$

$$= 25\,\mathrm{cm}\ \text{(to two significant figures)}$$

Q2

(a) The light pendula gain energy from the heavy pendulum; this is transferred through the supporting string.

(b) The light pendulum that gains most energy (the one that swings with greatest amplitude) is the same length as the heavy pendulum.

(c) The light pendulum that is the same length as the heavy one will eventually swing in step with the heavy one, but it may take some time for this situation to become established.

(d) The other pendula swing at the same frequency, but their oscillations are out of step (out of phase) with those of the heavy one.

Q3

You should have observed that there were more equal amplitudes of vibrations for all the driven pendula and that the whole arrangement comes to rest sooner than with the small weights.

Q4

Most musical instrument bodies need to be heavily damped so that they quickly stop vibrating at one frequency as the player plays the next. Some instruments are designed to be lightly damped to sustain the note just played even while others are played afterwards. Pianos have foot pedals that allow the player to control the amount of damping by bringing dampers into contact with the strings.

Swings require light damping to prolong the ride.

Car suspensions need to be fairly heavily damped, otherwise the passengers would soon be violently travel sick when going over a bumpy road!

Q5

If it approached the reflection point as a crest then it was reflected as a trough, if it approached as a trough then it was reflected as a crest – i.e. its phase was reversed.

Q6

(a) The horizontal component of the tension in the pendulum string.

(b)

$$F = ma$$

$$= -\left(\frac{mg}{l}\right)x$$

therefore

$$a = -\left(\frac{g}{l}\right)x$$

(c)

$$a = -(2\pi f)^2 x$$

Since

$$a = -\left(\frac{g}{l}\right)x$$

$$\frac{g}{l} = (2\pi f)^2 \qquad (3.4)$$

therefore

$$f = \frac{1}{2\pi}\sqrt{\frac{g}{l}}$$

As

$$T = \frac{1}{f}$$

$$T = \frac{1}{\frac{1}{2\pi}\sqrt{\frac{g}{l}}}$$

$$= 2\pi\sqrt{\frac{l}{g}}$$

Q7

(a) $x_0 = 1.0\,\text{m}$ when $t = 0$

$x = 0.50\,\text{m}$ when $t = 1.0\,\text{s}$

$x = x_0 \cos(2\pi ft)$

$f = \dfrac{1}{2\pi t} \cos^{-1}\left(\dfrac{x}{x_0}\right)$

$\quad = \dfrac{1}{2\pi\,\text{s}} \cos^{-1}(0.50)$

$\quad = 0.167\,\text{Hz}$

$\quad = 0.17\,\text{Hz}$

(b)

$v = 2\pi f x_0 \sin(2\pi ft)$

$\quad = 2\pi \times 0.167\,\text{Hz} \times 1\,\text{m} \times \sin(2\pi \times 0.167 \times 1)$

$\quad = 0.910\,\text{ms}^{-1}$

(c)

$\text{time taken} = \dfrac{\text{period}}{4}$

$\quad = \dfrac{T}{4}$

$\quad = \dfrac{l}{4f}$

$\quad = 6\,\text{s}$

Q8

$k = -\dfrac{F}{x}$

$\quad = -\dfrac{2000\,\text{N}}{30 \times 10^{-3}\,\text{m}}$

assuming $g = 10\,\text{ms}^{-2}$

$k = 6.67 \times 10^4\,\text{N}\,\text{m}^{-1}$

$F = ma$

$\quad = -kx$

therefore

$a = -(2\pi f)^2 x$

$\quad = -\dfrac{kx}{m}$

(*Note:* We would normally write $a = -(2\pi f)2x_0$ as this represents maximum acceleration, which occurs at maximum displacement or amplitude. Here we have used x instead, as we began by using the expression $F = -kx$.)

Therefore

$(2\pi f)^2 = \dfrac{k}{m}$

so

$f = \dfrac{1}{2\pi}\sqrt{\dfrac{k}{m}}$

$\quad = \dfrac{1}{2\pi}\sqrt{\dfrac{6.67 \times 10^4\,\text{N}\,\text{m}^{-1}}{1000\,\text{kg}}}$

$\quad = 1.3\,\text{Hz}$

We are now going to examine sounds from musical instruments. You will know from looking at a jazz or pop group, or particularly a symphony orchestra, that most of the instruments can be divided up into three main types: string, wind and percussion. These may be, for example, guitars or double-basses, flutes or trumpets, and drums or vibraphones.

In this section we will look at the ways in which these different instruments produce sounds of different pitch and loudness, and at why different instruments have their own special sound that enables you to identify them.

You will find this section easier to follow, and more fun, if either you or someone else in the physics group has experience of playing a stringed or wind instrument.

READY TO STUDY TEST

Before starting this section you should make sure that you are familiar with the work covered in Sections 2 and 3.

QUESTIONS

R1 If a wave has a wavelength, λ, of 0.500 m and it is travelling at a velocity, v, of 100 m s^{-1}, what is the frequency, f, of the wave?

R2 The wavelength, λ, of a particular wave is 1.0 m and its frequency, f, is 50 Hz. How long does it take this wave to travel 1.0 km?

R3 A mass, m, of 0.10 kg hanging from a spring is pulled down 0.05 m and released so that it oscillates up and down about its original (at rest) position with a frequency, f, of 0.50 Hz.

(a) What is the periodic time, T, of the oscillation?

(b) If the period of oscillation of a mass, m, on a spring is given by:

$$T = 2\pi\sqrt{\frac{m}{k}}$$

What is the spring constant, k, for the spring?

R4 Waves are described in terms of wavelength, velocity, frequency and amplitude. One of these cannot be changed by the medium through which the wave is travelling.

(a) Which cannot be changed, and what determines its value?

(b) How are each of the others changed?

4.1 Stringed instruments

Stringed instruments are used to produce musical sounds by putting energy into a length of string or wire that is fixed at both ends and has a certain **tension** on it. Figure 4.1 shows the layout of a basic stringed instrument called a sonometer, which you may have in your laboratory. As you have seen in Section 3.4, a stationary wave is set up in the string as it vibrates at its natural frequency.

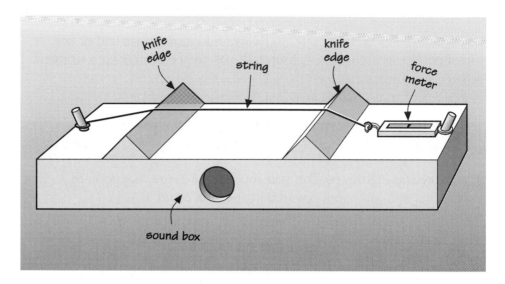

Figure 4.1
A basic stringed instrument

You can produce sounds with a sonometer by setting its string vibrating in the same way as a guitar (plucking) or a double-bass (scraping) or even a piano (hitting).

The plucking, scraping or hitting are just different ways of putting energy into the string to make it move to produce the sound.

 Either from your own experience or by carefully inspecting any stringed instruments that you are able to borrow from the music department, can you suggest what three different properties of the stretched string can be varied in order to change the sound coming from the vibrating string?

You can change the length, the tension and the **mass per unit length** (a combination of density and thickness).

Exploration 4.1   Seeing string vibrations

Apparatus:

◆ sonometer   ◆ strobe light

The string on an instrument vibrates much faster than the eye can see. This exploration uses a stroboscope light source instead of a continuous source such as the Sun or room lighting. The strobe light flashes on and off at a precisely controlled frequency and by adjusting this frequency close to the vibration frequency of the plucked string (or a multiple of it), you will be able to see the string apparently vibrating very slowly. You will need to do this experiment in a darkened room, or at least shield the wire from direct light.

If you have the time, you may like to try observing tuning forks illuminated by a strobe light with its flash frequency adjusted to the frequencies of the various tuning forks.

All participants and observers should wear safety spectacles or goggles for this exploration. Any stretched material may cause serious eye injury if it snaps. Strobe lights can cause epileptic fits in some people. Do not look directly into the flashing strobe light – view the string from the side of it. Do not turn the frequency of the strobe below 20 Hz.

10
MINUTES

Exploration 4.2
Properties affecting the vibrations of a string

All participants and observers should wear safety spectacles or goggles for this exploration. Any stretched material may cause serious eye injury if it snaps.

Apparatus:

◆ sonometer   ◆ set of tuning forks   ◆ microphone   ◆ amplifier   ◆ frequency meter

Part (i) The effect of string length

40
MINUTES
plus analysis

You need to know the frequency of the plucked sonometer string. You can choose one of two alternative methods to find this.

You can use a set of calibrated tuning forks that have their frequency of vibration engraved on them, and tune the plucked string by varying only its length (its tension must be kept constant throughout this part of the experiment) until it is in unison with the chosen tuning fork. It is a good idea to strike the prongs of the fork on a rubber block rather than on any hard surface. You could select about five or six different, evenly spaced, tuning fork frequencies to tune your string to. The alternative electronic method is shown in Figure 4.2 overleaf.

In this arrangement, choose a set of five or six well-spaced lengths of the sonometer string. Keep the string tension constant throughout the experiment. Set the string vibrating and pick up the sound vibrations with the microphone, which is connected to the frequency meter. You may need to connect an amplifier between the microphone and frequency meter.

Arrange your results ito a suitable table and include a column of calculated values of 1/(string length) in cm^{-1}.

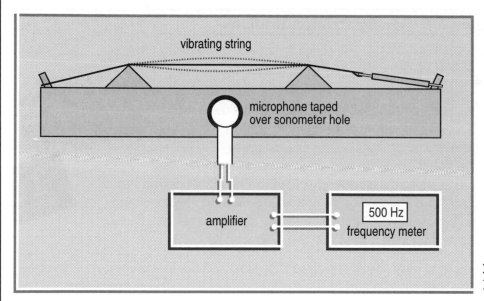

Figure 4.2
Electronic method

Now plot two graphs from these results. The first with frequency on the *y*-axis and string length on the *x*-axis, and the second with frequency again on the *y*-axis and 1/(string length) on the *x*-axis.

 When you've plotted both of these and discussed their shapes in your group, you should decide which of the two graphs tells you most easily what is the mathematical relationship between the frequency produced by a vibrating string and its length.

You should decide that $f \propto 1/\text{length}$ as it gives a straight line going through the origin.

Part (ii) The effect of string tension

20 MINUTES plus analysis In this part you must keep the length of vibrating string at a constant value and change the tension (since this is the variable property you are now interested in).

In your group, devise a suitable scheme to investigate the effect of changing the tension by using the sonometer. You can find the string frequency using either the tuning forks or the frequency meter.

When you've got five or six sets of frequency and corresponding tension values, try plotting two graphs once more: both with frequency on the *y*-axis, but one with tension on the *x*-axis and the other with the square root of tension on the *x*-axis.

 Which of these two graphs tells you most directly what the mathematical relationship is between the frequency of a vibrating string and its tension?

Again it's the straight-line relationship of the second graph that tells you that there is a direct proportionality between frequency and square root of tension, i.e.

$$f \propto \sqrt{\text{tension}}$$

Part (iii) The effect of string material

You will know that it is easy to move small masses about, but much more difficult to move large masses. Using this knowledge, develop a simple theory about how a set of strings that are identical in every way except for their mass per unit length will vibrate when they are plucked. Test your theory experimentally.

You need to use two or more strings on the sonometer that are made from different density materials, or from the same material but with different cross-sectional areas. If you find it is not possible to arrange this with apparatus available in your laboratory then the home-made apparatus shown in Figure 4.3 will do just as well.

Measure the average mass per unit length of each string. Discuss in your group, and perhaps with your teacher, ways of doing this accurately without using a lot of the material or chopping it into bits. Then make sure that all the strings are exactly the same length between the knife-edge bridges or the metal pipes, and that the tension on each one is exactly the same. Now pluck each string and find its frequency by using your frequency meter as in part (i). Tabulate your measurements of string frequency and corresponding mass per unit length (gm^{-1}) and include a column of

$$\sqrt{\frac{1}{\text{mass per unit length}}}.$$

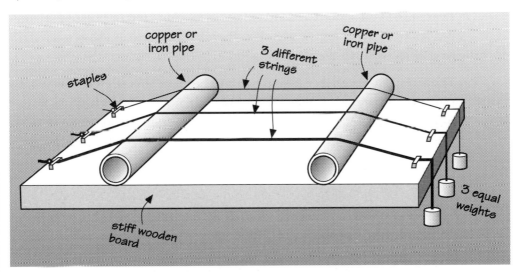

Figure 4.3 An arrangement for Exploration 4.2 (iii)

Your experimental results from Exploration 4.2 should have demonstrated how the frequency of vibration of a string fixed at both ends depends on the three properties you investigated, and the exact mathematical dependence of the frequency on each of these properties. In fact these can be summarized in a single expression:

$$\text{frequency} \propto \frac{1}{\text{length}} \times \sqrt{\frac{\text{tension}}{\text{mass per unit length}}}$$

In symbols this is:

$$f \propto \frac{1}{l} \times \sqrt{\frac{T}{\mu}}$$

where μ is used to represent the mass per unit length.

You have now spent a lot of time and effort on a series of experiments investigating the production of sounds by a vibrating string. We suggest that one or two groups now write up the experiments in the form of a scientific paper to present as a short lecture to the whole physics group. (Your teacher may be able to show you an example of a scientific paper.) You will need to prepare diagrams, tables of results and graphs on overhead projector transparencies to assist with your story. You might like to finish with a critical discussion on the uncertainties and reliability of the experiments.

4.2 Vibration of strings

Every time you started a string vibrating by plucking or banging it you put some strain energy into it. You then let it vibrate at its own natural frequency until all the vibrational energy was dissipated.

The string stores energy (strain energy) because it is stretched when it is plucked or banged. The amount of stored energy depends upon how much it is stretched and the material of the string. The Young modulus, E, is the property of the material involved, where

$$E = \frac{\text{stress}}{\text{strain}}$$

Stress is defined by the force per unit area of cross-section. Strain is defined by the extension per unit length.

So

$$\text{stress} = \frac{F}{A}$$

and

$$\text{strain} = \frac{x}{l}$$

where F is the stretching force (the increase in the tension), l and A are the string's length and cross-sectional area, respectively, and x is the extension of the string.

This gives

$$E = \frac{F/A}{x/l}$$
$$= \frac{Fl}{xA} \qquad (4.1)$$

The strain energy stored is given by the work done in stretching the string, i.e.

$$\text{strain energy} = \frac{1}{2}Fx \text{ (or average force} \times \text{distance moved)} \qquad (4.2)$$

Since $F = 0$ when $x = 0$ the average stretching force as the string is stretched is $\frac{1}{2}F$.

Rearranging Equation (4.1)

$$F = \frac{EA}{l}x$$

So Equation (4.2) can be written as

$$\text{strain energy } = \frac{EA}{2l}x^2$$

Q1 What happens to this vibrational energy of the string as the sound dies away after the string is first energized? Try to be specific about where the transfers are occurring. ◆

You will have noticed by now that a string fixed at both ends cannot vibrate freely at any frequency, but does so at very precise and fixed frequencies. These are known as its **resonant frequencies**.

A striking example of the power of **resonance** was provided by the Tacoma Narrows suspension bridge in the USA. In 1940, a very strong wind oscillated the bridge at its resonant frequency. The amplitude of the oscillation became so large that the four-month-old bridge was torn apart.

The remains of the Tacoma Narrows suspension bridge

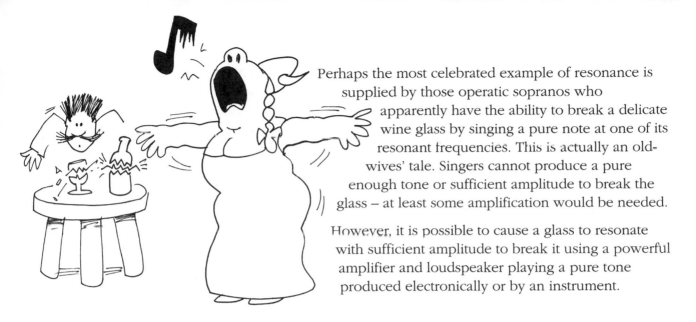

Perhaps the most celebrated example of resonance is supplied by those operatic sopranos who apparently have the ability to break a delicate wine glass by singing a pure note at one of its resonant frequencies. This is actually an old-wives' tale. Singers cannot produce a pure enough tone or sufficient amplitude to break the glass – at least some amplification would be needed.

However, it is possible to cause a glass to resonate with sufficient amplitude to break it using a powerful amplifier and loudspeaker playing a pure tone produced electronically or by an instrument.

4.3 Patterns of string vibrations

So far you have found that the vibrational frequency produced by a fixed string is governed by just three factors. There is in fact a fourth factor, which is a property of how the string vibrates: its **vibrational mode**. Figure 4.4 shows you some of the different ways in which a string can vibrate even with a fixed length, tension and mass per unit length.

Key terms to note in this figure are **harmonic** and **fundamental**.

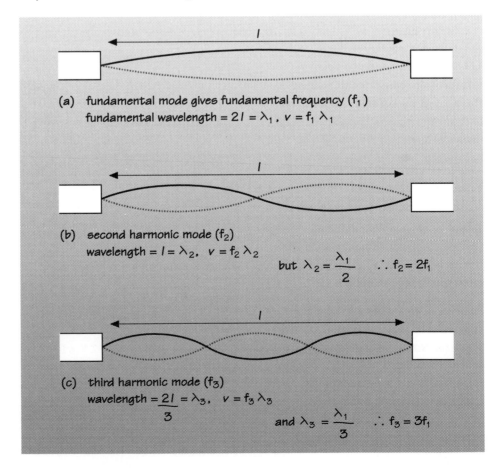

(a) fundamental mode gives fundamental frequency (f_1)
fundamental wavelength $= 2l = \lambda_1$, $v = f_1 \lambda_1$

(b) second harmonic mode (f_2)
wavelength $= l = \lambda_2$, $v = f_2 \lambda_2$
but $\lambda_2 = \dfrac{\lambda_1}{2}$ $\therefore f_2 = 2f_1$

(c) third harmonic mode (f_3)
wavelength $= \dfrac{2l}{3} = \lambda_3$, $v = f_3 \lambda_3$
and $\lambda_3 = \dfrac{\lambda_1}{3}$ $\therefore f_3 = 3f_1$

Figure 4.4
Vibrational modes of a string

The important thing to understand about a vibrating string is that it vibrates not only at its lowest or fundamental frequency, but at many higher frequencies (which are called harmonics) as well. We tend to notice only the fundamental frequency as the majority of the energy put into a string is usually used to produce the fundamental vibration frequency, while much less is used in exciting the higher harmonics.

So what about these higher harmonics if we don't notice them? Well, it's not that we don't hear them, we do, but we don't notice them directly as separate sounds. The higher harmonics are actually heard mixed up with the fundamental. This combined sound, as represented by the complicated looking waveforms you were seeing on the oscilloscope in earlier experiments, is recognized by your brain (when it interprets the electrical signal sent from the ear) as the special **quality** or **timbre** of the particular string that helps you to distinguish between guitars, pianos, violins or double-basses.

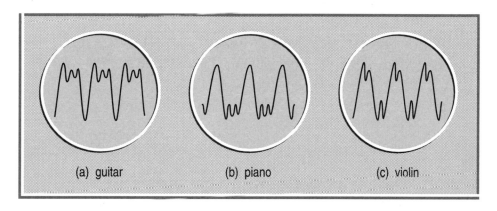

(a) guitar   (b) piano   (c) violin

Figure 4.5
Waveforms of the same note played by different instruments

See how well you can distinguish between instruments: get one member of the physics group to make a tape recording of different stringed instruments and then play it to the rest of the group so that they can try to identify them.

If your laboratory has harmonic analysing software for a computer you could now analyse the waveforms of different stringed instruments.

Professional violinists like Nigel Kennedy can excite a string to produce its second or third harmonic, instead of its fundamental, by lightly touching the bowed string where a **node** should appear (a point along the length of the string where the string does not actually vibrate). (In Figure 4.4(b) there is a node half-way along the string as well as at each end.) Copy Figure 4(a) and (b), then:

(a)   draw an arrow on Figure 4.6(a) at the point on the string where Nigel would lightly place his finger to excite the second harmonic

(b)   draw an arrow on Figure 4.6(b) to show where he would place his finger to excite the third harmonic.

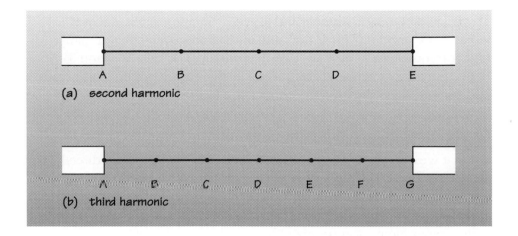

Figure 4.6
Second and third harmonics

(a) second harmonic

(b) third harmonic

(a) The second harmonic is twice the fundamental frequency, so there should be a node half-way along the string. Nigel would touch the string at C.

(b) The third harmonic has a wavelength that is a third of the wavelength of the fundamental. Therefore Nigel's finger would be at C or E.

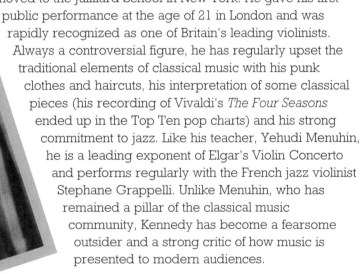

NIGEL KENNEDY: A VIOLINIST WITH A DIFFERENCE

Nigel Kennedy can be regarded as the *enfant terrible* of violinists. Born in Brighton in 1956, he studied the piano and then the violin at the world famous Yehudi Menuhin School at Stoke d'Abernon in Surrey. He then moved to the Juilliard School in New York. He gave his first public performance at the age of 21 in London and was rapidly recognized as one of Britain's leading violinists. Always a controversial figure, he has regularly upset the traditional elements of classical music with his punk clothes and haircuts, his interpretation of some classical pieces (his recording of Vivaldi's *The Four Seasons* ended up in the Top Ten pop charts) and his strong commitment to jazz. Like his teacher, Yehudi Menuhin, he is a leading exponent of Elgar's Violin Concerto and performs regularly with the French jazz violinist Stephane Grappelli. Unlike Menuhin, who has remained a pillar of the classical music community, Kennedy has become a fearsome outsider and a strong critic of how music is presented to modern audiences.

4.4 Wind instruments

These instruments produce their sounds not by vibrating a part of the instrument itself but by vibrating a column of air trapped inside the tubing of the instrument.

The methods used to excite the trapped air column into vibration fall into three main types (see Figure 4.7):

1 lip vibrations or 'raspberry' tones (used, for example, with trumpets and trombones)

2 clamped reed vibrations (used, for example, with saxophones, clarinets and bassoons)

3 edge tones or eddy vibrations (used, for example, with recorders, flutes and organ pipes).

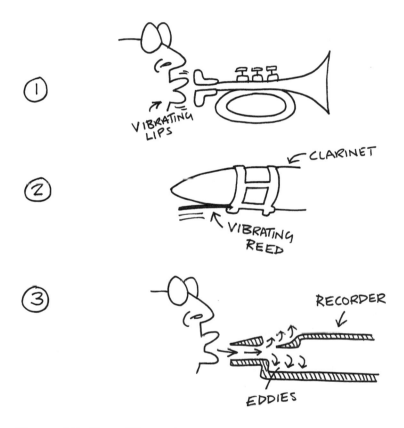

Figure 4.7 How different instruments vibrate air columns

Try to borrow an instrument of each type from the music department and have a go at playing each of them.

In order to investigate how air vibrates in columns in the laboratory you can excite the vibrations by using a tuning fork or the paper cone of a loudspeaker fed from a signal generator to whack the air molecules at the end of the columns.

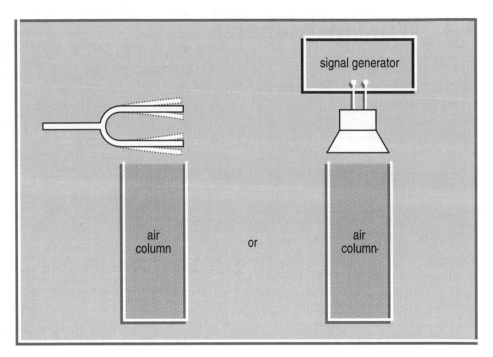

Figure 4.8
Exciting air columns

Although you can use these methods to make the air column vibrate to some extent at the frequency dictated by the tuning fork or loudspeaker you will find that as you change the driving frequency you will reach some special values at which the loudness of the sound produced by the air column is greater than at most of the other frequencies you have used. This occurs when the air column vibrates at one of its own natural frequencies, i.e. it resonates. The air columns used in wind instruments come in two types, depending on how the air is restricted by the metal, plastic or wood tube that encloses it: there are **open pipes** (the flute and one type of organ pipe) and **closed pipes** (the clarinet, the other type of organ pipe and swanee whistles). Both types of pipe have at least one open end (see Figure 4.9).

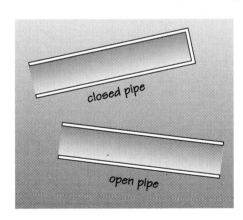

Figure 4.9 Open and closed pipes

Exploration 4.3   Seeing how air resonates in a column

Apparatus:

◆ wide glass or plastic tube, 1 m long ◆ Sellotape ◆ Plasticine
◆ cork – ground into very small pieces ◆ small loudspeaker
◆ signal generator ◆ metre rule ◆ large cork

50 MINUTES

You will see in Figure 4.10 that the air column is of fixed length
and is horizontal. It is wedged securely with Plasticine to prevent rolling
and then Sellotaped to the bench. It is important to minimize the vibration of
the glass – the Plasticine should help with this.

Fix a cork securely into one end of the tube and place the small loudspeaker at the other
end so that its paper cone faces into the tube and is about 3 mm away from the open end
of the tube. Set the signal generator to give a sine wave and the amplitude to low. Switch
on the signal generator and adjust its output so that you can only just hear the sound
from the loudspeaker between the frequencies of about 200 Hz and 1000 Hz. Turn the
frequency control to about 700 Hz and steadily decrease the frequency until you hear an
increase in loudness. At this point, slightly vary the frequency up and down

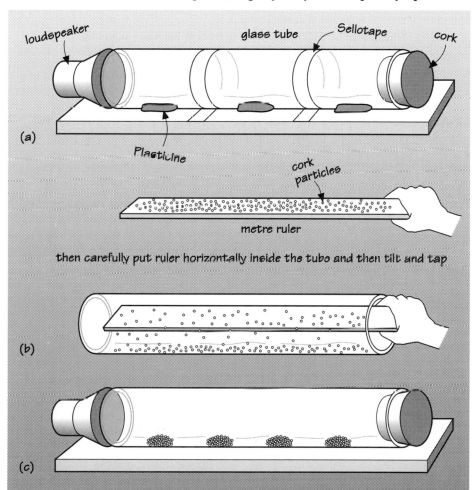

Figure 4.10
Experimental set-
up for resonating
air investigation

until you are sure you are hearing the loudest sound; you now have the air column vibrating at one of its own resonant frequencies. Turn the signal generator output down to zero but do not switch it off. Lay an even line of ground cork along the whole length of a metre rule. Place this inside the glass tube and tap it so that the cork particles fall on to the tube bottom as shown in Figure 4.10(b). Now, with one end stoppered and the loudspeaker fixed at the other, turn the signal generator output up to its maximum. Watch the behaviour of the cork particles for the next few seconds, or for as long as your ears or your partner's can stand the noise. Switch off the signal generator and note that the cork has rearranged itself into small piles with gaps in between where there is almost none at all (see Figure 4.10c). If you see smaller piles within the larger ones, these are due to the glass vibrating as well as the air it contains. Measure the average distance between the cork piles and make a note of the tube's resonant frequency (the signal generator frequency).

Remove the bung from the end and empty out all the cork. Without replacing the bung, refix the tube to the bench. Start with the signal generator frequency at about 700 Hz and slowly reduce it until the loudness increases as before. Slightly adjust the frequency until you are sure you are hearing the loudest sound. You are now hearing one of the resonant frequencies of the tube, but this time it is for an open pipe. Turn the signal generator output to zero.

Place an even line of ground cork along the inside of the tube and arrange the loudspeaker as before. Turn up the signal generator to full output for a few seconds and the cork will rearrange itself again. Measure the distance between the piles of cork and note the signal generator frequency.

Q2 Why does the cork sit in piles at certain fixed places along the tube when the air column inside is resonating? Discuss this with your partners. ◆

To help in your analysis you could find a different, lower, resonant frequency in the tube, put in more cork and see how it rearranges itself when that frequency note is sounded loudly in the tube. You should find that the little piles of cork are evenly spaced again.

The ground cork will be at rest only if the air immediately surrounding it is almost still. This means that there is a fixed pattern of air vibration amplitude along the tube. A standing or stationary wave has been set up. This is a type of wave in which the positions of maximum and zero amplitude of vibration do not change.

A standing wave in the tube can be thought of as being formed as follows. The air is forced to vibrate at the same frequency as the loudspeaker diaphragm, since this diaphragm is in direct contact with the air molecules at the end of the tube. When the diaphragm pushes towards the end of the tube, a compressed layer of air is produced at this point. On the other half cycle of the diaphragm's movement, as it moves away from the tube end, a decompressed or rarefied layer of air is produced (see Figure 4.11).

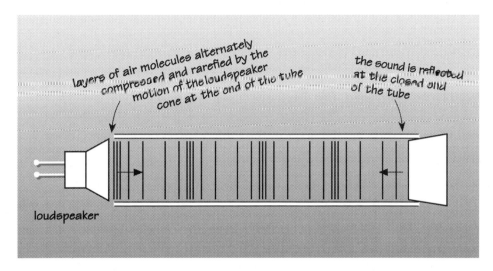

Figure 4.11
Compressions and rarefactions of air in a tube

The compression or rarefaction will then travel down the tube to the far end where it will be reflected back up the tube to meet the loudspeaker diaphragm, which is still moving. If the wave arrives back at the loudspeaker so that the movement of the air particles is in step with the movement of the loudspeaker's diaphragm the air column is resonating.

Most types of musical instrument produce their sounds from stationary wave vibrations.

The speed at which the compressions or rarefactions travel up and down the tube is the speed of sound in air.

E Exploration 4.4   The speed of sound in free air

40 MINUTES

Apparatus:

◆ two pieces of wood planking, about 25 cm long   ◆ three or four stopwatches
◆ sports tape measure

The basic idea of this experiment is very simple: a short, sharp sound is made, it travels to a wall and is reflected back to its origin. The speed at which the sound travels can be calculated by timing its journey there and back and measuring the distance it has travelled.

It sounds simple enough, but you need to do some careful preparation to achieve a good value.

First, you need to find a large open area, free from obstacles that might give unwanted echoes, and with a high wall at one end. The distance from the wall to the opposite end of the open area should be about 100 m. If it is more the timing will be easier and more reliable – the reverse will apply for a shorter distance.

You can make a loud and sharp sound by smartly hitting the two pieces of wooden planking together.

You need to work in groups. As many people as possible should do the timings to obtain a reasonable average, several could measure the distances and one should make the noise and record the results. Remember to write a report of this experiment when you've finished.

Now you know how fast the compressions and rarefactions travel up and down the air columns in the tubes.

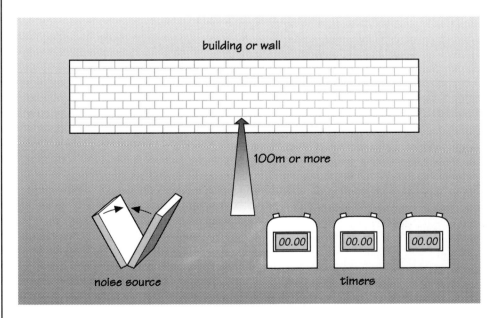

Figure 4.12   A suggested arrangement for Exploration 4.4

Q3 Bats find their food by echo location, which is similar to the method you have just used in Exploration 4.4. They emit a rapid series of ultrasound squeaks (frequencies beyond the top end of the range of human hearing) to bounce off flying insects in the surrounding air. If the time between adjacent squeaks is 50 ms, what is the farthest distance at which an insect can be clearly detected by a bat? (The speed of sound in air at 20 °C is 343 m s^{-1}.)

Discuss with your partners why the bat had this maximum clear detection distance. How could the bat ensure that it did not hear echoes from farther away than this? ◆

There is an interesting article on bat echo location in *New Scientist* magazine (Vol. 143, No. 1942) that you may like to read.

4.5 Pipe frequencies

You can now investigate the properties of an air column that affect its resonating frequencies. From your experience of seeing and hearing wind instruments, you will be aware that short instruments, such as a piccolo or a descant recorder, tend to produce high-pitched notes, while long ones, such as a trombone, produce lower-pitched notes. So, the length of the air column is obviously important. (You can learn more about this in the SLIPP unit *Physics for Sport*.)

Another property of a gas column (this time inside your own sound producing equipment of mouth, nose and throat) that affects the sound frequencies it produces is shown by the following example. Deep-sea divers speak with a high-pitched squeaky voice while breathing an atmosphere with a high helium content. This 'heliox' breathing mixture is about 1/7th the density of ordinary air. So this suggests that gas density in the column is important. (You can learn more about this in the SLIPP unit *Physics for Sport*.)

 Considering a molecular model of a gas, what properties of a gas or a mixture of gases can you change, and in what way, so that its density will change?

Density will increase if the molecular mass increases and/or if the intermolecular distance decreases.

Apparatus:

◆ wide glass or plastic tube, 1 m long   ◆ water reservoir   ◆ rubber tubing
◆ set of tuning forks or loudspeaker and signal generator   ◆ metre rule
◆ two clamps

This exploration uses a similar tube to the one used in Exploration 4.3. This time the tube is clamped vertically and the lower part is filled with water. The amount of water in the tube can be altered by raising or lowering the water reservoir attached to the second clamp, as shown in Figure 4.12.

Glass tubes must have smooth ends, and should be handled with care and secured safely. Wear safety spectacles or goggles.

You can excite vibrations in the air column as you did before by using either a tuning fork or a small loudspeaker about 1 cm above the open end of the tube. The sound source should only just be audible, so you need to do this experiment in a quiet laboratory.

45 MINUTES

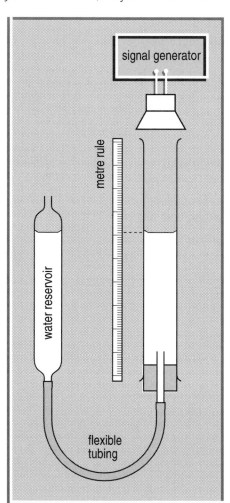

Choose a frequency near 500 Hz and, with the initial water level near the top of the tube, gradually lower the water until you hear an increase in loudness. You can find the precise level by slightly adjusting the height of the reservoir until you get the position of maximum loudness. At this point, measure the length of the air column from the water surface to the top of the tube.

Try repeating this procedure for four more resonant frequencies between 500 Hz and 250 Hz.

Tabulate these measurements, including a column of 1/length values, and plot graphs of frequency against length and frequency against 1/length.

You should now be able to deduce the relationship between the frequency of a resonating air column and its length by looking for the straight-line relationship. Draw the best straight line that fits the data. It may not go exactly through the origin, but you should ignore this slight deviation from direct proportion.

You should discover the same sort of relationship here as you found for the string length in Exploration 4.2.

Figure 4.13   Resonance tube experiment

But, you may ask, how well does this work for real wind instruments?

Exploration 4.6   Measuring frequencies using real instruments

Apparatus:

◆ microphone   ◆ amplifier   ◆ frequency meter
◆ wind instruments

If you have access to some real wind instruments, then you can investigate how frequency depends on the length of the air column. The only difficulty you may find is how to measure the tube length if you choose to work on a member of the brass family. One of the simpler instruments to work on is a descant recorder.

You can find the frequency of any note experimentally by playing into a microphone connected to a frequency meter. The length of the resonating air column is from the sharp blade at the top, which produces the eddy currents, to the first open hole down the instrument, as shown in Figure 4.14.

45 MINUTES

There is a risk of damaging equipment by handling connectors and wires incorrectly when making connections to the signal generator, loudspeaker, etc. Follow the points below when undertaking this exploration.
1   Make sure all the equipment is switched off whilst setting up the circuit.
2   All connectors and the loudspeaker terminals must be insulated. Do not use bare connectors such as 'spade' connectors or crocodile clips.
3   Switch off before making any physical adjustments to the circuit.

The only other requirement is that the player must know which note on the musical scale they are playing. If none of your group has any musical knowledge of the instrument you are using, you now need to do a bit of literary research in the library or music department to find out the note produced by a particular fingering.

All you have to do is to play a steady note and find its frequency and the tube length that produced it. Try this for several different notes and record your measurements in a table. If, as Exploration 4.5 suggested, $f \propto 1/\text{length}$, then a graph of these two values should be a straight line through the origin.

If you have access to a variety of wind instruments you could test them all in this way. You could then have an interesting discussion about where the end of the tube is in a bell-ended instrument.

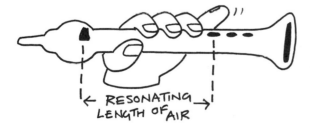

Figure 4.14   Using a descant recorder

Exploration 4.7 Overblowing to produce overtones

10 MINUTES

Apparatus:

◆ wind instrument(s) ◆ Sellotape

You can do this experiment with a recorder, a trumpet or a trombone if you have these available. If you use the trumpet or trombone, you must not press the valves or use the slide. With the recorder, stick pieces of Sellotape over the first five holes on the upper side and over the thumb hole underneath.

Recorder method

Blow gently but steadily down the mouthpiece to produce the lowest note you can, then increase the strength of your blowing until a new but higher-pitched note is produced. With even harder blowing you should be able to produce a still higher note, and if you make a supreme blowing effort then you may achieve an even higher note!

Trumpet or trombone method

The lowest-pitched note is produced with a minimum tension of the lips and minimum blowing effort. The higher-pitched notes are produced by blowing harder and increasing the lip tension.

Overblowing, then, is another method of changing the frequency at which the air in a pipe resonates. How does this work?

The sound compressions and rarefactions you make at the mouthpiece go down the pipe and reflect at the far end. They travel at a fixed speed, which depends upon the gas.

Now, the speed of sound equals the frequency of the sound multiplied by its wavelength, as you discovered in Section 2.4. Therefore, if the wave frequency generated in the pipe can be increased by overblowing, then the corresponding wavelength must have been decreased. Also, only specific frequencies can be produced by a pipe of a particular length. So what is going on?

When faced by a novel problem it is often useful to see if you have come across anything of a similar nature before. This may give you a good start in explaining the new problem. Using this idea, you will recall that a string of fixed length and tension could be made to resonate at a series of different fixed frequencies (higher harmonics) – look at Figure 4.4 again.

Q4 How do you think the sound waves arrange themselves in the resonating pipes to give the different frequency notes you heard? You may like to discuss your ideas with other students.

Illustrate your answer by drawing displacement–position graphs to represent sound waves in the pipes. See Figure 4.15 for an example.

Remember:

■ at the end of the tube where the sound vibrations are being produced with maximum energy input, the air molecule vibration amplitude will be a maximum

■ at an open end of a tube there is no restriction on the vibration of the air molecules, so a maximum vibrational amplitude could occur here as well

■ at a closed end of a tube the air molecules cannot vibrate at all because of the incompressibility of the solid end. ◆

Figure 4.15
Representing longitudinal waves as displacement-position graphs

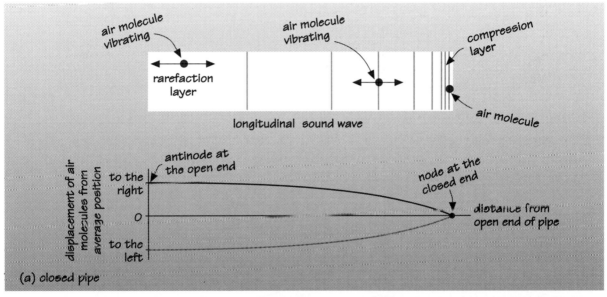

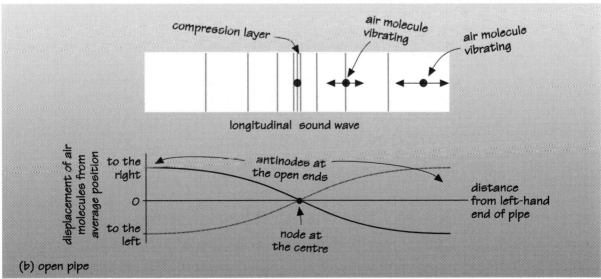

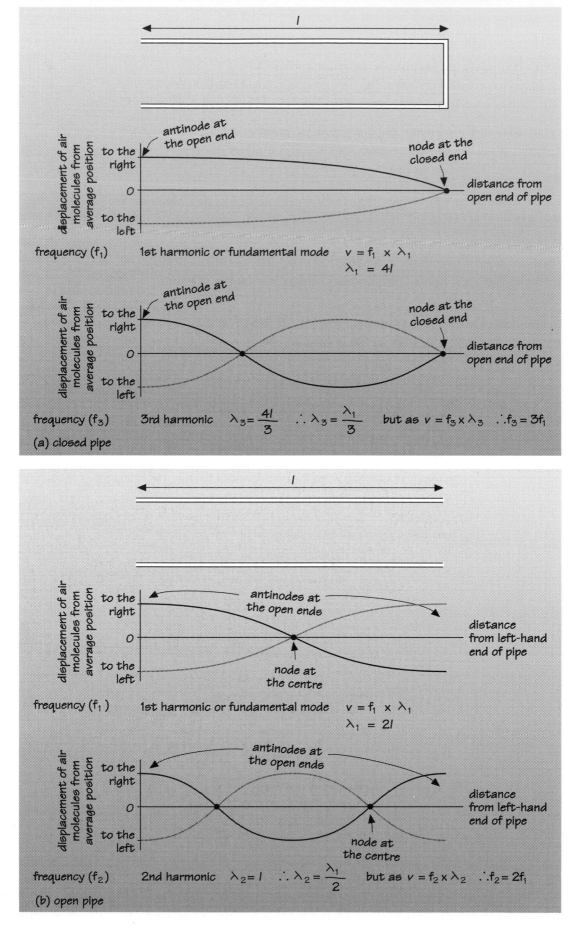

Figure 4.16 Vibrational modes of open and closed pipes

4.6 Patterns of pipe resonances

So now you've got three factors that can affect the frequency of the note produced by a pipe – the length, the gas it contains and how hard you blow. Two of these are properties of the air column itself and the third is the vibrational mode set up. Figure 4.16 shows some of these vibrational modes for each type of pipe.

 How do you think the air pressure along the pipe will vary when a pipe is resonating? Remember what happens to the pressure of a gas when it is compressed or rarefied (decompressed).

The pressure changes will be maximum at the nodes and zero at the **antinodes** (see Figure 4.17)

You will remember the way in which a string vibrates when excited: like a string, a resonating air column vibrates not only at the fundamental frequency but at higher harmonics as well. You hear the fundamental as the dominant sound with smaller amounts of the higher harmonics added to it.

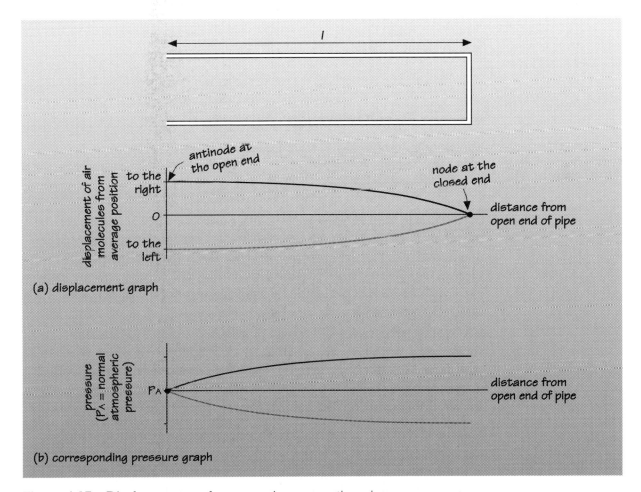

Figure 4.17   Displacement and pressure in a resonating pipe

As with stringed instruments mentioned in Section 4.3, when a wind instrument plays a single note, the special property of the sound you hear (the combination of the pipe's fundamental frequency plus little bits of higher harmonics) is called the quality or timbre of the sound. Physicists refer to this as a sound's **harmonic content**.

4.7 Pipe end corrections

You may have been wondering how the air in a resonating pipe stops vibrating right at the open end of the pipe. Surely there is little restriction on contacting the air molecules outside the end of the pipe. This would extend the length of resonating air column! Well, of course, this is what actually happens in all wind instruments, and you can carry out an experiment to find out by how much the resonating extends beyond the limit of the pipe itself.

The amount of resonating air sticking out beyond the actual pipe is found experimentally to be about $0.6 \times$ the tube radius.

In Figure 4.18(a)

$$\frac{\lambda}{4} = l_1 + e \tag{4.3}$$

and in Figure 4.18(b)

$$\frac{3\lambda}{4} = l_2 + e \tag{4.4}$$

where e is the **end correction**.

Subtracting Equation (4.3) from Equation (4.4) will give

$$\frac{2\lambda}{4} = l_2 - l_1 \tag{4.5}$$

So, if you start with two pipes, one a little more than three times longer than the other (three times the shorter pipe plus at least one diameter should do), you can carry out an experiment to find the end correction, which will be the same in both pipes if they have the same radius. The shorter pipe is played in its fundamental mode using a loudspeaker connected to a signal generator. By starting from a low frequency and gradually increasing it, the fundamental frequency can be found. The longer pipe is then tuned, by gradually shortening it, until it resonates at the same frequency as the short pipe. Only a little movement should be needed. The longer pipe is then playing its third harmonic. Now you have l_1 and l_2. Use these to find λ from Equation (4.5) and substitute this value into Equation (4.3) or (4.4) to find the end correction, e.

This method would, however, give an inaccurate value because of all the experimental errors. Exploration 4.8 involves plotting a straight-line graph that is the best fit to several scattered points; this smoothes out the effects of experimental errors and results in a more accurate value.

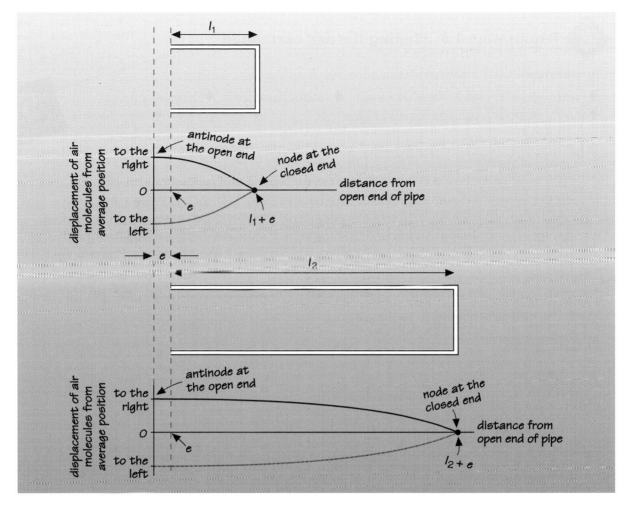

Figure 4.18 End corrections in a resonating pipe

◆E◆ Exploration 4.8 Finding the end correction

Apparatus:

- ◆ wide glass or plastic tube, 1 m long ◆ water reservoir ◆ rubber tubing
- ◆ tuning fork or loudspeaker and signal generator ◆ metre rule ◆ two clamps

50 MINUTES

Set up the apparatus as for Exploration 4.5 (see Figure 4.13) and start with a sound frequency somewhere near 500 Hz. Lower the water level from near the top of the pipe until you hear an increase in loudness and measure the first resonance position. Continue to lower the water level until you hear another increase in sound level and measure this new position, which is the position of the second resonance. (You will find that the air column for the second resonance is approximately three times the length of the air column for the first resonance.) If you repeat this procedure for four or five lower frequencies and tabulate your results of frequencies, first resonant length and second resonant length, you can then find both the end correction for your pipe and the speed of sound in the air column.

At first resonance

$$l_1 + e = \frac{\lambda}{4}$$

using

$$\lambda = \frac{v}{f}$$

$$l_1 + e = \frac{v}{4f}$$

so

$$l_1 = \frac{v}{4f} - e$$

which can be rewritten as

$$l_1 = \frac{v}{4} \times \frac{1}{f} - e \qquad\qquad (4.6)$$

In a similar way, an equation relating length and frequency at the second resonance can by produced, i.e.

$$l_2 = \frac{3v}{4} \times \frac{1}{f} - e \qquad\qquad (4.7)$$

Equations (4.6) and (4.7) represent straight-line relationships between measured resonant air-column lengths and the reciprocal frequencies. So if you plot graphs of length (on the y-axis) against $1/f$ (on the x-axis) for l_1 and again for l_2, then the gradients will give you values of $v/4$ for the first resonance line and $3v/4$ for the second resonance line. These will allow you to calculate the speed of sound in air in your laboratory.

You should find that the two lines cross the length axis at the same point on its negative part. The value of the length at this point is the value of the end correction of your pipe.

You have now used two quite different methods for measuring the speed of sound in air in this section (Explorations 4.4 and 4.8).

Q5 Which of these two methods do you think gives you the most reliable value for the speed of sound in air? Try to support your decision by looking at the accuracy with which you measured the time of the echoes and then compare it with the accuracy with which you could measure the air column lengths.

You might like to discuss this with your partners and your teacher. ◆

The following questions are quite demanding, you are likely to need some help to answer them fully, accurately and efficiently. Ask a teacher for assistance or work with other students.

If you have the chance to visit a factory that makes wind instruments you will discover that the sizes of the different instruments are not worked out from theoretical principles at all. The calculations involved would be very complicated, as the instruments themselves are very complex. For example, not only does the column of air extend beyond the end of the instrument, there is usually a bell shape at that end of the tube as well. In addition, many wind instruments do not have a uniform bore.

Q6 Two students stretch a piece of rubber cord between them. Its original length was 2.5m and they manage to stretch it by 2.0m. The elastic constant of the cord is $100\,\mathrm{Nm^{-1}}$. The mass of the cord is 300g.

What is the speed at which a transverse wave could travel along the cord,

given the expression $v = \sqrt{\dfrac{T}{\mu}}$?

(The meanings of the terms can be found in the preceding text.) ◆

Q7 An organ pipe (open at one end) is 5.00m long and is producing sound at its second harmonic. What is its fundamental frequency? (Take the speed of sound to be $343\,\mathrm{ms^{-1}}$ and ignore any end correction.) ◆

Q8 The natural frequency, f, of a taut string is given by:

$$f = \frac{1}{2l}\sqrt{\frac{T}{\mu}}$$

A particular string is found to have a fundamental frequency of 200Hz. If the tension is doubled what is the new fundamental frequency? (The meanings of the terms can be found in the preceding text.) ◆

Q9 If instead of doubling the tension, the length of the string is increased by exactly 1 per cent, what would the new frequency be? (*Note:* The mass of the string has not changed.) ◆

Q10 Calculate the force required to produce a strain of $\dfrac{1}{1000}$ in a steel wire with a diameter of 1.00mm. What is the energy stored in the wire if it is 1.00 m long?

(Young modulus, E, for steel $= 2.0 \times 10^{11}\,\mathrm{Nm^{-2}}$.) ◆

Achievements

After working through this section you should be able to:

- name some common examples of sound producers in the three classes of musical instruments

- explain how changing the length, tension or mass per unit length of a string fixed at both ends can change the musical note it produces

- identify patterns of resonance in a vibrating string and state which harmonic or overtone you are seeing

- relate the frequency of a particular string resonance to its fundamental frequency

- describe three methods of producing vibrations in the air columns of musical instruments

- explain the difference between an open pipe and a closed pipe and give examples of musical instruments of each type

- explain what a resonating system is and give some common examples of them

- identify patterns of resonance in a vibrating air column and state which harmonic or overtone you are seeing

- explain how changing the length of a pipe or the density of the gas filling a pipe can change the musical note the pipe produces.

Glossary

Antinode   The point along the length of a string of maximum amplitude of vibration of the string.

Closed pipe   A pipe or tube effectively open at one end only.

End correction   The distance that a resonating column of air extends beyond the end of the pipe that actually contains it.

Fundamental   The lowest resonant frequency of a vibrating string or air column.

Harmonic content   The fundamental and higher harmonic frequencies that are added together to make a particular musical sound.

Harmonic   One of the natural vibration frequencies of a string or air column.

Node   A point along the length of a string where the string does not actually vibrate.

Mass per unit length   The ratio of the mass of a string or wire to its length, often expressed in $kg\ m^{-1}$

Open pipe   A pipe or tube effectively open at both ends.

Overblowing   The technique by which a player selects resonant frequencies higher than the fundamental frequency of a wind instrument by increasing the air flow through or across it.

Quality   A musical term for the harmonic content of a musical sound. (See *timbre.*)

Resonance   Vibration at the resonant frequency of a system.

Resonant frequency   A natural frequency of vibration of a system that is absorbing small amounts of energy from an outside periodic force to maintain large amplitudes of vibration.

Tension   A longitudinal force applied to a string to keep it taut.

Timbre   A musical term for the harmonic content of musical sound. (See *quality.*)

Vibrational mode   One of the patterns of vibration of a resonating system.

Answers to Ready to Study test

R1

$$v = f\lambda$$

so

$$f = \frac{v}{\lambda}$$

$$= \frac{100\,\mathrm{m\,s^{-1}}}{0.50\,\mathrm{m}}$$

$$= 200\,\mathrm{Hz}$$

R2

$$v = f\lambda$$

$$= 50\,\mathrm{Hz} \times 1.0\,\mathrm{m}$$

$$= 50\,\mathrm{m\,s^{-1}}$$

$$t = \frac{s}{v}$$

$$= \frac{1 \times 10^3\,\mathrm{m}}{50\,\mathrm{m\,s^{-1}}}$$

$$= 20\,\mathrm{s}$$

R3

(a)

$$T = \frac{1}{f}$$

$$= \frac{1}{0.5\,\mathrm{s^{-1}}}$$

$$= 2\,\mathrm{s}$$

(b)

$$T = 2\pi\sqrt{\frac{m}{k}}$$

so

$$k = \left(\frac{2\pi}{T}\right)^2 m$$

$$= \left(\frac{2\pi}{2\,\mathrm{s}}\right)^2 \times 0.1\,\mathrm{kg}$$

$$= 0.99\,\mathrm{kg\,s^{-2}}$$

R4

(a) Frequency cannot be changed, it is fixed by the vibrating source of the wave.

(b) The wavelength changes if the velocity of the wave changes; this would occur if the wave moved into a medium with different properties.

The velocity of a particular wave depends upon particular properties of the medium through which it is travelling. For example, waves in liquids have different velocities in liquids of different densities or depths; the velocity of a wave in a string depends upon the tension in the string and the mass per unit length of the string; and the velocity of light depends upon the density of the transparent material it is travelling through.

Amplitude is a measure of the amount of energy in a wave. Inevitably waves lose energy as they travel and so the amplitude decreases.

Answers to questions in the text

Q1

The string's vibrational energy is transferred to vibrational energy of the surrounding air and vibrational energy of the string's supports.

The molecules in the air and the supports are made to vibrate more, which causes a small rise in their temperature.

Q2

The particles of ground cork are so light that they are easily moved by small vibrations of the air molecules in the tube, so they are blown to positions where the air is not vibrating. These positions are called vibration nodes.

Q3

The bat needs to receive the echo from an insect before it emits the next squeak if it is not to be confused by multiple echoes. Therefore the maximum time available for clear detection is 50 ms. In this time the sound has to go from bat to insect to bat again, so the time taken for the sound to reach the insect must be no more than 25 ms.

Distance travelled by the sound

$$= 343.4 \, \text{m s}^{-1} \times (25 \times 10^{-3}) \, \text{s}$$
$$= 8.6 \, \text{m}$$

The bat can control the distance over which its echo location operates by controlling the loudness of its squeaks, so that echoes from more than 8.6 m away are too quiet for the bat to hear.

Q4

See Figure 4.15. The lowest note you produced was the fundamental, followed by the second harmonic and, if you could manage it, the third harmonic.

Q5

First you need to look at the uncertainties in the measurements you made for each of the two experiments. Then calculate the percentage uncertainty for each measurement you took and see which is the largest. This is the dominant uncertainty for your method of finding the sound velocity.

Discuss this exercise thoroughly with your teacher.

Q6

$$T = kx$$
$$= 100 \, \text{N m}^{-1} \times 2.0 \, \text{m}$$
$$= 200 \, \text{N}$$
$$l = 4.5 \, \text{m}$$

$$\mu = \frac{m}{l}$$
$$= \frac{0.300 \, \text{kg}}{4.5 \, \text{m}}$$

$$v = \sqrt{\frac{T}{\mu}}$$
$$= \sqrt{\frac{200 \, \text{N}}{0.300 \, \text{kg} / 4.5 \, \text{m}}}$$
$$= 54.8 \, \text{m s}^{-1}$$
$$= 55 \, \text{m s}^{-1} \text{ (to two significant figures)}$$

Q7

For the second harmonic of a closed pipe

$$l = \frac{3}{4} \lambda_2$$
$$= \frac{3}{4} \frac{v}{f_2}$$

so

$$f_2 = \frac{3}{4} \frac{v}{l}$$
$$f_1 = \frac{f_2}{3}$$
$$= \frac{v}{4l}$$
$$= \frac{343 \, \text{m s}^{-1}}{4 \times 5.00 \, \text{m}}$$
$$= 17.2 \, \text{Hz}$$

Q8

$$f' = \frac{1}{2l}\sqrt{\frac{T'}{\mu}}$$

$$= \frac{1}{2l}\sqrt{\frac{2T}{\mu}}$$

$$= \sqrt{2} \times \frac{1}{2l}\sqrt{\frac{T}{\mu}}$$

$$= \sqrt{2} \times f$$

$$= \sqrt{2} \times 200\,\text{Hz}$$

$$= 283\,\text{Hz}$$

Q9

$$l' = \frac{101}{100} \times l$$

$$\mu = \frac{m}{l}$$

therefore

$$\mu' = \mu \times \frac{100}{101}$$

therefore

$$f' = \frac{1}{2l'}\sqrt{\frac{T}{\mu'}}$$

$$= \frac{100}{101} \times \frac{1}{2l}\sqrt{\frac{101}{100}\frac{T}{\mu}}$$

$$= \frac{100}{101}\sqrt{\frac{101}{100}} \times f$$

$$= \sqrt{\frac{100}{101}} \times 200\,\text{Hz}$$

$$= 199\,\text{Hz}$$

Q10

$$E = \frac{F/A}{x/l}$$

So

$$F = E\left(\frac{x}{l}\right)A$$

$$= E\left(\frac{x}{l}\right)\pi r^2$$

$$= 2.0 \times 10^{11}\,\text{N m}^{-2} \times \frac{1}{1000} \times \pi \times (0.50 \times 10^{-3}\,\text{m})^2$$

$$= 157\,\text{N}$$

$$= 1.6 \times 10^1\,\text{N (to two significant figures)}$$

Energy stored $= \frac{1}{2}Fx$

$$x = \frac{Fl}{EA}$$

So

energy stored $= \frac{F^2 l}{2EA}$

$$= \frac{(157\,\text{N})^2 \times 1.0\,\text{m}}{2 \times 2.0 \times 10^{11}\,\text{N m}^{-2} \times \pi \times (0.50 \times 10^{-3}\,\text{m})^2}$$

$$= 7.85 \times 10^{-2}\,\text{J}$$

$$= 7.9 \times 10^{-2}\,\text{J (to two significant figures)}$$

In this section you will carry out some graphical and mathematical exercises. Graphical methods are very important in the interpretation of experimental data, and no physicist can avoid algebra!

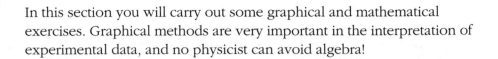

READY TO STUDY TEST

Before you begin this section you should be able to:

- rearrange equations to make a particular term the subject of the equation
- plot experimental data as a straight-line graph so that particular quantities can be found from the gradient and/or the intercept of the graph (this was introduced in Section 4)
- give an explanation of the term 'elastic'
- define the Young modulus, E (covered in Section 4.2).

You should be able to explain the following:

- $y = mx + c$ is the general linear expression
- if an experiment produces data in the form of corresponding values for x and y they can be plotted as a straight-line graph
- if the data pairs (x, y) are plotted on a graph so that y-values are given on the ordinate (vertical) axis and x-values on the abscissa (horizontal) axis, then m in the general expression is the gradient and c is the intercept
- the gradient is the slope of the graph, i.e. the ratio of the change in y to the change in x
- the intercept is the value of y when the value of x is zero, i.e. the value of y where the graph crosses the y-axis if it is drawn at $x = 0$.

You should also be able to describe simple kinetic theory, in particular:

- the equation of state of a gas, $pV = nRT$, and the meaning of the terms
- the equation $\dfrac{P_1 V_1}{T_1} = \dfrac{P_2 V_2}{T_2}$
- the differences between gases, liquids and solids at the molecular level.

(Simple kinetic theory is considered in the SLIPP unit *Physics for Sport*.)

QUESTIONS

R1 Rearrange the following equations to make the **bold term** the subject

(a) $v = \boldsymbol{f}\lambda$

(b) $v = f\boldsymbol{\lambda}$

(c) $y = mx + \boldsymbol{c}$

(d) $y = m\boldsymbol{x} + c$

(e) $s = \boldsymbol{u}t + \frac{1}{2}at^2$

(f) $s = ut + \frac{1}{2}\boldsymbol{a}t^2$

R2 A graph shows the position of a vehicle as a function of time. It is a straight-line graph with the position plotted on the vertical axis. The gradient of the graph is the steady speed of the vehicle

(a) If the position is 2000 m at 10.0 s and 1000 m at 100 s, what is the steady speed of the vehicle?

(b) At what time is the position zero?

R3 A student carries out a simple experiment on a gas. The gas is compressed in stages, the volume, V, and the pressure, p, are measured at each stage. How should the student plot the data to show that $pV = $ constant?

R4 One of the largest concert halls in London at the start of the jazz era was the Exeter Hall, whose dimensions were 40.0 m long by 23.0 m wide by 16.0 m high. What mass of air did it contain when empty (density of air at 20 °C is 1.38 kg m^{-3}) and when full (1400 audience, 80 member orchestra and a chorus of 420)? Assume that the size of each person is equivalent to a box measuring 1.60 m tall by 40 cm wide by 20 cm deep. (Density = mass/volume or $\rho = m/V$)

R5 Children playing with a bicycle pump, of maximum volume 300 cm^3, find that they can squash air. When blocking the end with a finger they can push the handle two-thirds of the way in. What is the highest pressure that they can produce? Take air pressure as 1×10^5 Pa and assume that the temperature is constant.

R6 Briefly list the differences between solids, liquids and gases using simple kinetic theory ideas. You could arrange the information in a table using headings such as: particle arrangement, interparticular separation, interparticular forces, type of particle motion, etc.

5.1 Velocity of a wave in a string

Exploration 5.1   Velocity of a wave in a string

Apparatus:

- signal generator ◆ audio vibrator ◆ thin string or thread
- small weights (20 g, 10 g) ◆ small pulley

All participants and observers should wear safety spectacles or goggles for this exploration. Any stretched material may cause serious eye injury if it snaps. Put a cardboard carton on the floor under the weights to keep your feet out of the way in case the wires break

30
MINUTES
plus analysis

Set up the apparatus as you did in Exploration 3.4, but without the strobe light. Use the apparatus to obtain values for the wavelength of a stationary wave in the string at different signal generator frequencies – i.e. slowly increase the frequency from the signal generator until a stationary wave is set up, measure the wavelength (in Figure 3.10, for example, the wavelength is approximately 2/3 of the length of the string) and read the frequency on the signal generator scale.

Make sure you have at least five reliable data points.

Now, think about how you can plot the data to produce a straight-line graph, from the gradient of which you can find the velocity of the travelling waves in the string.

The important equations are:

$$y = mx + c \tag{5.1}$$

the general linear expression, and

$$v = f\lambda \tag{5.2}$$

Clearly, you need to rearrange Equation (5.2) so that v is in the position that corresponds to m in Equation (5.1). This can be done by making either f or λ the subject. It is usual to make the variable in the position corresponding to y the **dependent variable**, i.e. the one that changes as a result of changing another – in this case f is being changed, which causes λ to change, so λ is the dependent variable.

Q1 (a) Rearrange Equation (5.2) to make λ the subject.

(b) What terms in the rearranged equation correspond to y, x, m and c in the general linear expression? ◆

Check your answer with the one given at the end of this section.

Now, calculate the values that must be plotted on the abscissa of your graph and plot the points.

The points are unlikely to lie exactly on a straight line. Draw in the best straight line, so the points are scattered evenly about it.

Determine the gradient of the line by taking full advantage of the scales – don't just use a small part of the graph.(See Figure 5.1.)

So, what is the velocity of waves in your string?

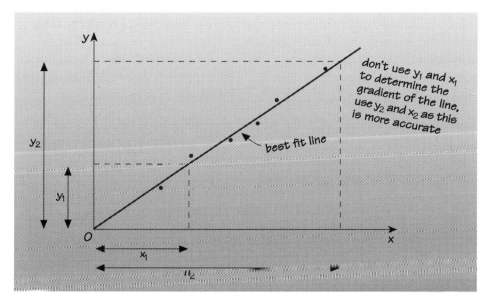

don't use y_1 and x_1 to determine the gradient of the line, use y_2 and x_2 as this is more accurate

best fit line

Figure 5.1
Drawing a best fit line and finding its gradient

5.2 Velocity of a sound wave in air

As you found in Section 2.4, the relationship

$$v = f\lambda$$

applies to all waves and does not depend upon any of the properties of the medium or the type of wave being considered.

When a sound wave travels through any medium, that medium is alternately compressed and expanded. You might therefore reasonably expect that properties affecting the motion of particles of the medium, and the forces on them, will affect the velocity of the wave. In other words, it is reasonable to suppose that the properties of a medium will affect the value of v, but not the relationship between v, f and λ.

In a simplified model you could suggest that just two properties affect the motion of and the forces on the particles:

1   the elastic property of the medium

2   the inertial property of the medium's particles.

The elastic property should determine the squeeziness of the medium and so the **bulk modulus**, K, might be tried. (This is the three-dimensional equivalent of the Young modulus, which is one-dimensional, see Section 4.2.)

One **inertial** property (something that would determine how easy it is to move the particles) you might consider is the density, ρ.

It is then possible to derive the equation

$$v = \sqrt{\frac{K}{\rho}}$$

If the medium is a gas it can be squeezed in two main ways: **isothermally**, when the gas is compressed sufficiently slowly that it does not change temperature during a change of volume, and **adiabatically**, where the gas is compressed rapidly so that its temperature changes because of the energy transfer brought about by the work done in compressing it.

At sound wave frequencies, the gas through which the sound travels is found to undergo adiabatic expansions and compressions. Under these conditions the bulk modulus $K = \gamma P$, where γ is a constant for the gas concerned and P is the gas pressure.

The equation for the speed of sound in the gas now becomes

$$v = \sqrt{\frac{\gamma P}{\rho}}$$

Incidentally, Sir Isaac Newton got this wrong. He assumed that isothermal changes were taking place and predicted much lower values for the speed of sound in air than those measured in experiments.

If you are a wind instrumentalist you may be surprised that the temperature of the gas does not appear in the velocity equation, as you will know that a rise in air temperature (as may happen during a jazz concert in a nightclub) will change the pitch of an instrument. However, both the pressure and the density are changed when the temperature changes.

Q2 (a) A piper accidentally sits on the bag of his bagpipes, effectively sealing it and trapping 2500 cm³ of air inside. By what percentage will the air pressure inside the bag increase as the air temperature rises from 17°C to normal body temperature (37°C)? Assume that the bag is made from incompressible material and that the air pressure inside the bag before sealing was at 1×10^5 Pa.

(b) By how much will the density of the air change during this time? ◆

It is most important that wind instrument makers make allowance for change of temperature in their designs.

Q3 To see how the change of pitch comes about you need to combine the equation of state of a gas (ideal) with the two sound velocity equations. Work through the following maths for yourself.

Using simple **kinetic theory**,

$$PV = nRT \tag{5.3}$$

$$v = \sqrt{\frac{\gamma P}{\rho}} \tag{5.4}$$

$$v = f\lambda \tag{5.5}$$

$$\rho = \frac{M}{V} \tag{5.6}$$

If M is the molar mass then the number of moles, n, equals 1. So Equation (5.1) simplifies to

$$PV = RT$$

and then rearranges to

$$P = \frac{RT}{V}$$

Substitute this expression for P into Equation (5.4).

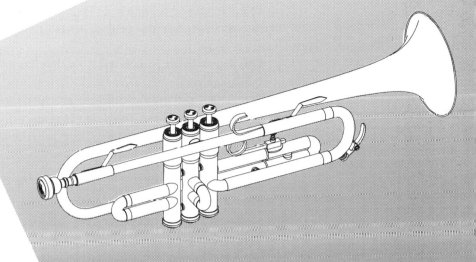

Figure 5.2
A trumpet

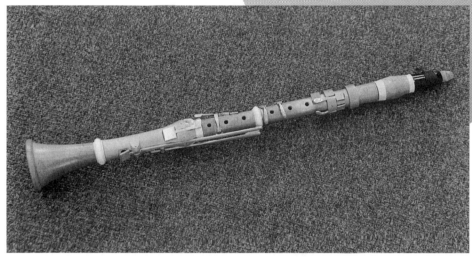

Figure 5.3
A clarinet

Now use Equation (5.6) to substitute for r in your expression for v, and simplify the result.

The final equation should clearly show that v does depend upon temperature. Check your answer with the one given at the end of this section. ◆

In this equation, γ, R and M are fixed constants that do not change with temperature, so the dependence of v on T is

$$\frac{v}{\sqrt{T}} = \text{constant}$$

so

$$\frac{v_1}{\sqrt{T_1}} = \frac{v_2}{\sqrt{T_2}}, \text{ etc.}$$

Don't forget that gas law temperatures are measured on the absolute scale of temperature in kelvins and not in degrees Celsius.

When a flautist plays a fixed note, the fingering allows an air column of a fixed length to resonate. So what sort of frequency change is going to occur when this air column heats up?

Q4 A jazz flautist plays a C note that has a frequency of 262Hz using an air column length of 65.0cm (including an end correction of 5.00 cm – see Section 4.7) when the air in a nightclub is a coolish 15.0°C. The air heats up to an amazing 38.0°C as the night goes on. What frequency will the flautist produce using the same fingering as at the start of the evening?

Of course a professional player will adjust the length of the resonating air column by moving the tuning barrel. By how much will the player need to adjust the tuning barrel to make sure that the instrument is still in tune at the end of the evening? You can assume that the speed of sound at the cooler temperature is 343 m s^{-1}. ◆

5.3 Velocity of sound in a solid

The particle arrangement in a solid is much tighter than the very spaced out particles in a gas. This means that the interparticular forces are very much stronger and when a section is compressed or stretched by a vibration this motion will be rapidly relayed to the rest of the solid. For simplicity, the motion of the particles can be considered to be one-dimensional.

Waiting for the train!

A good illustration of one-dimensional sound vibrations travelling through a solid can be seen in many old Wild West films, as shown in this cartoon.

So, in our simplified version of the velocity equation, the bulk modulus can be replaced by its one-dimensional cousin, the Young modulus (E).

Therefore

$$v = \sqrt{\frac{E}{\rho}}$$

Q5 Use the figures given in Table 5.1 to calculate the speeds of sound in steel and spruce. ◆

Table 5.1 Values of the Young modulus and density for steel and spruce

	Steel	Spruce
E/Pa	2.1×10^{11}	1.4×10^{10}
ρ/kg m^{-3}	7.8×10^{3}	6.0×10^{2}

In Section 4.1 you were able to show, from the results of three experiments, that the fundamental resonant frequency, f, of a string is related to the length of the string, l, the tension in the string, T, and the mass per unit length of the string, μ, as follows:

$$f \propto \frac{1}{l}\sqrt{\frac{T}{\mu}}$$

in full

$$f = \frac{1}{2l}\sqrt{\frac{T}{\mu}}$$

This could be confirmed by further experiments.

When the string is vibrating in its fundamental mode

$$\lambda = 2l$$

so

$$f = \frac{1}{\lambda}\sqrt{\frac{T}{\mu}}$$

or

$$f\lambda = \sqrt{\frac{T}{\mu}}$$

As

$$v = f\lambda$$

it follows that

$$v = \sqrt{\frac{T}{\mu}}$$

Q6 You now need the co-operation of your music department. Borrow one each of the four violin strings (G, D, A, E) and measure their mass per unit length. Next, on a tuned violin, measure the length of each from where they cross the nut just beyond the tuning pegs to where they meet the bridge and compare it to the values you can calculate from the data given in Table 5.2. Calculate the tension needed in each string to allow it to produce its fundamental frequency. You will see how well-designed the instrument is; it is very light and fragile looking, but it has to be extremely strong to withstand these tensions. ◆

Table 5.2 Typical characteristics of violin strings

String	G	D	A	E
Frequency/Hz	196	293	440	660
Wave speed/m s^{-1}	125	188	282	422
Mass per unit length/kg m^{-1}				
Tension/N				

Achievements

After working through this section you should be able to:

- define the terms 'adiabatic' and 'isothermal'

- accurately make substitutions into an equation

- explain how the temperature affects the performance of a wind instrument

- state and use the relationships $\dfrac{v_1}{v_2} = \sqrt{\dfrac{T_1}{T_2}}$ for a gas, and $v = \dfrac{T}{\mu}$ for a string.

Glossary

Adiabatic   This term describes the compression or expansion of a gas when there is no energy transfer at all with the surroundings. Hence the gas does not heat the surroundings and the surroundings do not heat the gas. This type of change occurs when pressure changes are very rapid, as with the passage of a sound wave, where temperature changes occur locally within the gas itself.

Bulk modulus   The force per unit area that must be applied to a material to produce a change in volume of one unit. As it is related to volume, it is three-dimensional. Young's modulus is the force per unit area that must be applied to produce a change in length of one unit, so it is one-dimensional. Both are properties of the material.

Dependent variable   Only one variable should be changed at a time by an experimenter, a second variable (which can be measured) might change as a result of the experimenter's actions on the first variable. The second variable, which depends upon the first variable, is called the 'dependent' variable.

Isothermal   Gas pressure changes in which heat energy is allowed into or out of the gas in order to keep its temperature constant.

Inertia   Objects do not change their motion unless they are subjected to forces – this is because of their inertia. Mass gives a measure of inertia.

Kinetic theory   A simple theory that assumes that gas molecules have no volume and move randomly without losing kinetic energy as they collide with each other or the walls of their container.

Answers to Ready to Study test

R1

(a) $f = \dfrac{v}{\lambda}$

(b) $\lambda = \dfrac{v}{f}$

(c) $c = y - mx$

(d) $x = \dfrac{y - c}{m}$

(e) $u = \dfrac{s - \frac{1}{2}at^2}{t}$

(f) $a = \dfrac{2(s - ut)}{t^2}$

R2

(a)

$$\text{Gradient} = \frac{\text{change in position}}{\text{change in time}}$$

$$= \frac{1000\,\text{m}}{90\,\text{s}}$$

$$= 11.1\,\text{ms}^{-1}$$

(b)

$$\frac{\text{change in position}}{\text{change in time}} = \text{velocity}$$

so

$$\text{change in time} = \frac{\text{change in position}}{\text{velocity}}$$

$$= \frac{(2000 - 0)\,\text{m}}{11.1\,\text{ms}^{-1}}$$

$$= 180\,\text{s}$$

so the final time is 190 s.

R3

V is reduced and as a result p increases

$$p = \frac{\text{constant}}{V}$$

so the student should plot p on the ordinate (vertical axis) and $1/V$ on the abscissa (horizontal axis)

R4

Volume of the hall $= 40.0\,\text{m} \times 23.0\,\text{m} \times 16.0\,\text{m}$
$$= 14720\,\text{m}^3$$

As

mass = density × volume

mass of air $= 1.38\,\text{kg m}^{-3} \times 14720\,\text{m}^3$
$$= 20313.6\,\text{kg or } 20.3\text{ tonnes}$$

Approximate volume of a human
$$= 1.60\,\text{m} \times 0.40\,\text{m} \times 0.20\,\text{m}$$
$$= 0.128\,\text{m}^3$$

Total number of bodies $= 1400 + 80 + 420$
$$= 1900$$

so

total volume of bodies $= 1900 \times 0.128\,\text{m}^3$
$$= 243.2\,\text{m}^3$$

Volume of air in the hall now
$$= (14720 - 243.2)\,\text{m}^3$$
$$= 14476.8\,\text{m}^3$$

Mass of air now $= 1.38\,\text{kg m}^{-3} \times 14476.8\,\text{m}^3$
$$= 19977.98\,\text{kg}$$
$$= 19978\,\text{kg or } 20\text{ tonnes}$$

R5

$$\frac{P_1 V_1}{T_1} = \frac{P_2 V_2}{T_2}$$

so

$$\frac{1 \times 10^5\,\text{Pa} \times 300\,\text{cm}^3}{T_1} = \frac{P_2 \times \frac{1}{3} \times 300\,\text{cm}^3}{T_1}$$

therefore

$$P_2 = \frac{3 \times 1 \times 10^5\,\text{Pa} \times 300\,\text{cm}^3}{300\,\text{cm}^3}$$

$$= 3 \times 10^5\,\text{Pa}$$

R6

	Particle arrangement	Interparticular separation	Interparticular forces	Particle motion
Solid	Very regular	Very close	Very strong	Vibration only
Liquid	Long range order, partly regular	Fairly close	Weak	Vibration, rotation and slow translation
Gas	Completely random	Very far apart	Negligible	Very fast translation

Answers to questions in the text

Q1

(a) $\lambda = v/f$

(b) $y : \lambda$

$x : 1/f$

$m : v$

$c :$ zero

Q2

(a) Air temperature in the bag rises from 290 K to 310 K. Using the gas law equation for a fixed mass of gas being squashed

$$P_1 \times \frac{V_1}{T_1} = P_2 \times \frac{V_2}{T_2}$$

and putting in appropriate values you get

$$1 \times 10^5 \, \text{Pa} \times \frac{V_1}{290 \, \text{K}} = P_2 \times \frac{V_2}{310 \, \text{K}}$$

Remembering that $V_1 = V_2$, you then get

$$P_2 = 310 \times \frac{1 \times 10^5}{290} \, \text{Pa}$$

$$= 1.07 \times 10^5 \, \text{Pa}$$

The percentage rise is

$$\frac{(1.07 - 1.00) \times 10^5 \, \text{Pa}}{1.00 \times 10^5 \, \text{Pa}} \times 100 = 7\%$$

(b) Density = mass/volume

In this case neither the mass nor the volume changed, therefore there would be no change in gas density.

Q3

The substitution into Equation (5.4) should produce

$$v = \sqrt{\frac{\gamma RT}{\rho V}}$$

The substitution using Equation (5.6) should produce

$$v = \sqrt{\frac{\gamma RTV}{MV}}$$

Simplifying results in

$$v = \sqrt{\frac{\gamma RT}{M}}$$

Q4

First use the velocity and temperature equation to find the higher temperature velocity:

$$\frac{v_1}{v_2} = \sqrt{\frac{T_1}{T_2}}$$

i.e.

$$\frac{343 \, \text{ms}^{-1}}{v_2} = \sqrt{\frac{288 \, \text{K}}{311 \, \text{K}}}$$

$$= 0.962$$

$$v_2 = \frac{343 \, \text{ms}^{-1}}{0.962}$$

$$= 357 \, \text{ms}^{-1}$$

As the flautist uses the same fingering when it is hot as when it is cool, you can assume that the resonating air column is still 65 cm long. The flute is an open pipe instrument so its fundamental wavelength will be twice the resonating length, i.e. 1.30 m. You can now calculate the new frequency from

$$f = \frac{357 \, \text{m s}^{-1}}{1.30 \, \text{m}}$$

$$= 275 \, \text{Hz}$$

To retune the instrument to compensate for a rise in air temperature, the length of the resonating air column needs changing.

Therefore

$$\text{new wavelength} = \frac{357\,\text{ms}^{-1}}{262\,\text{Hz}}$$

$$= 1.36\,\text{m}$$

This is twice the air column length, therefore the new length = 68 cm, so the tuning barrel needs opening out by (68 − 65) cm = 3 cm.

Q5

$$\text{Speed in steel} = \sqrt{\frac{2.1 \times 10^{11}\,\text{Pa}}{7.8 \times 10^3\,\text{kg m}^{-3}}}$$

$$= 5190\,\text{m s}^{-1}$$

$$= 5.2\,\text{km s}^{-1}$$

$$\text{Speed in spruce} = \sqrt{\frac{1.4 \times 10^{10}\,\text{Pa}}{6.0 \times 10^2\,\text{kg m}^{-3}}}$$

$$= 4830\,\text{m s}^{-1}$$

$$= 4.8\,\text{km s}^{-1}$$

Q6

Different sets of violin strings will have varying values for their mass per unit length, depending on their manufacturer. Typical values are given in the table below, together with their corresponding tensions. Consult your teacher to check that your calculations are reasonable.

Typical characteristics of violin strings

String	G	D	A	E
Frequency/Hz	196	293	440	660
Wave speed/m s^{-1}	125	188	282	422
Mass per unit length/g m^{-1}	47	53	48	68
Tension/N	3	1.5	0.61	0.38

The path that sound follows from performer to audience is not uncomplicated.

How often can a musician play an instrument without the sound meeting obstructions? Even a good concert hall is full of them. And what happens when the sound of one instrument mixes with the sound of another, or it meets its own reflection?

You have probably seen demonstrations (or even carried out experiments yourself) of the behaviour of water waves in a ripple tank. These demonstrations illustrate most of the points listed in the Ready to Study test.

READY TO STUDY TEST

Before you begin this section you should revise earlier work on waves so that you can explain the following:

- straight (plane) water wave fronts become curved when they pass through a small gap: this effect is called diffraction

- the diffraction of the water waves is most pronounced when the size of the gap is less than the wavelength of the water waves

- if there are two gaps in a barrier placed in the path of the water waves, the emerging curved wave fronts will overlap and an interference pattern will been seen

- the interference pattern consists of lines of constructive and destructive interference: constructive where the two waves reinforce each other and destructive where the two waves cancel each other out, either partially or completely

- the interference pattern results from the different path lengths from the sources of the two waves

- if the two path lengths are equal, or the difference is a whole number of wavelengths, the interference is constructive because the two waves arrive in step (in phase)

- if the difference between the path lengths is an odd number of half wavelengths, the waves will at least partially cancel each other out because they will arrive out of step (in anti-phase)

QUESTIONS

R1 Draw the pattern you would see in a ripple tank if plane wave fronts encounter a small gap in a barrier set up parallel to the wave fronts.

R2 A ripple tank is set up as in Figure 6.1. What would happen at points A and B?

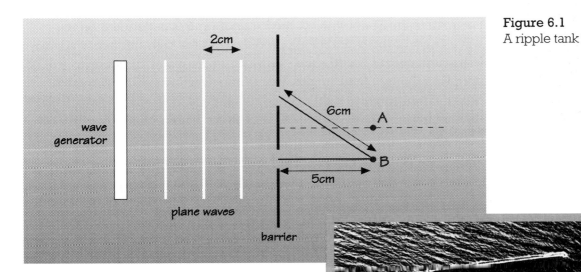

2cm

wave generator

6cm

A

5cm

B

plane waves

barrier

Figure 6.1
A ripple tank

6.1 Diffraction

Diffraction is the curving of the wave front of travelling waves when they are obstructed in any way – this results in the waves spreading

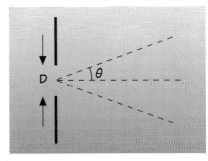

Water wave diffraction

out. You can see the effect when water waves pass through a gap in a barrier in a laboratory ripple tank or, on a much larger scale, at harbour entrances or round coastal promontories.

Sound waves from wind instruments and loudspeakers are diffracted at the edges of the hole at which they are produced (see Figure 6.2). As a consequence of this diffraction, not all the sound waves produced by an instrument or loudspeaker reach your ears in their original proportions. So people sitting in different positions at a concert will be hearing different sounds; however, they will still recognize the instruments being played.

The pattern of the diffraction is dependent on the size of the hole and on the wavelength of the sound wave being produced.

There is a cone of space in front of a loudspeaker aperture where the amplitude of the wave varies only a little.

The size of this cone is governed by the approximate relationship

$$\sin\theta \approx \frac{\lambda}{D}$$

where θ is the half-angle of the cone, D is the diameter of the aperture and λ is the wavelength of the sound produced.

Figure 6.2
Diffraction of sound at a circular aperture

For a fixed size of aperture D, the value of $\sin \theta$ is dependent on the wavelength of the sound being produced. So for high-frequency sounds less sound energy is diffracted sideways, whereas low frequencies will be diffracted through large angles. Jazz trumpeters and clarinettists often hold their instruments right out and swing them from side to side to allow their audience to hear the full effect of all the higher harmonics they are blowing!

Diffraction from the bell of a wind instrument actually varies in a far more complex way than that from a loudspeaker. There is plenty of scope for a research project here, to see, for example, how the quality of the sound changes as you listen from more oblique angles to the instrument's main axis.

LOUIS ARMSTRONG ('SATCHMO')

One of the all-time great black jazz musicians, Louis Armstrong was born in New Orleans in 1898 and died in New York in 1971. He started his career in about 1917 as a trumpeter and singer performing jazz on Mississippi river boats, and he formed his own band in the 1920s. His early recordings became world famous and had an enormous influence on the development of jazz. He was a brilliant trumpet player and his vocal contributions remain totally unmistakable, and led to him being given the nickname 'Satchelmouth' or 'Satchmo'. Armstrong is best remembered in this country through his appearances in many films and his great concert tours with his All Stars band in the late 1940s and the 1950s. Most of his recordings are still available and his most famous film appearance in *High Society* with Frank Sinatra and Bing Crosby is frequently on television. Louis Armstrong is certainly one of those musicians of whom one can say 'Once seen, never forgotten.'

In a concert hall or theatre, the cheaper seats may be behind large pillars that completely obscure the performers, but you can still hear the sound perfectly well. Suggest why this may be so.

Most of the wavelengths of the sound waves at a concert are about the same size as or greater than the pillar widths in concert halls, so the sound will be strongly diffracted round them. On the other hand, the wavelength of light is very much smaller than the pillar widths so light is not noticeably diffracted.

6.2 Interference

 Exploration 6.1

Apparatus:

◆ signal generator ◆ two loudspeakers
◆ power breaker plug

This experiment demonstrates what happens when sound waves from two sources meet. You need to connect two identical loudspeakers to a single signal generator, so that waves are produced **in phase**, and place them about 1 m apart, as shown in Figure 6.3. Choose a frequency of about 1000 Hz and adjust the sound so that it is quite loud but not painfully so. Now walk quietly about the laboratory as shown in the figure and listen carefully for changes in the loudness as you do so. You should find that the loudness of the sound depends upon your position in a very regular way. This effect is caused by the sound waves, one from each loudspeaker, meeting each other at different places in the laboratory. If you stand at a point where a compression from one loudspeaker meets a rarefaction from the other, you should hear no sound. In reality the situation is far more complex because multiple reflections from the floor, ceiling, walls and benches also contribute their share of sound at the point where you are standing, so the sound level isn't zero anywhere, but you will hear a considerable reduction in the level at some places.

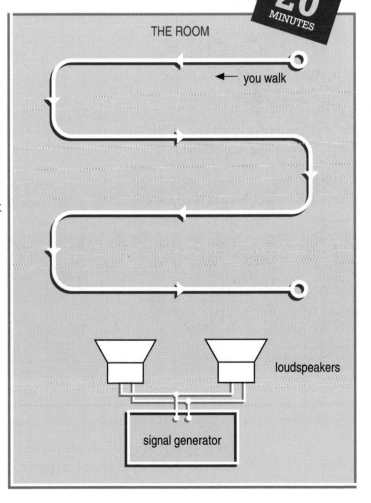

Figure 6.3
Experimental arrangement
for Exploration 6.1

Where a compression from one loudspeaker meets a compression from the other, the result is an extra large compression that thumps your eardrum extra hard. At this same place, some short time later, rarefactions from each loudspeaker will meet and your eardrum will be sucked out extra hard. So here the pressure at your eardrum fluctuates from very high to very low and you hear a louder than normal sound.

If this experiment is done out of doors on a still day, and well away from reflecting surfaces, then a very regular pattern of loudness and quietness can be found. You might like to discuss with your partners why you don't notice this effect at a concert.

This experiment is a sound wave analogue of Young's twin slit experiment with light waves, where the same theory can be used.

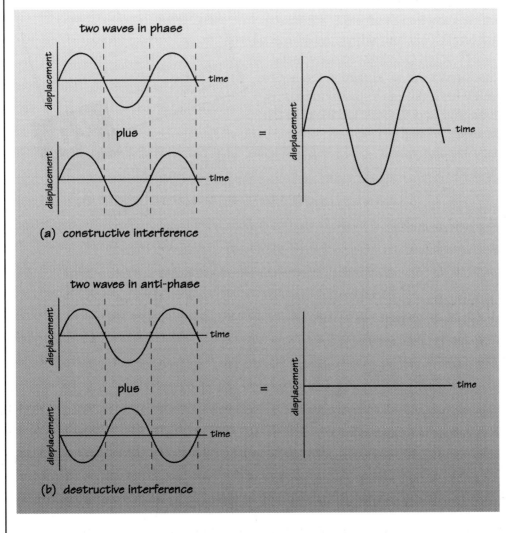

Figure 6.4 Constructive and **destructive interference** from two waves meeting

Q1 Two loudspeakers are placed 2.00m apart in the middle of a field and fed the same waveform from a signal generator operating at 2000Hz. What would you hear if your ear was 7.90m from one loudspeaker and 8.07m from the other? Take the speed of sound to be $343\,\mathrm{ms}^{-1}$. ◆

6.3 Beats

Beats are another effect that results from two sound waves meeting. This time the two sounds have different frequencies and roughly the same loudness. This effect is useful to musicians when an orchestra tunes up before a concert.

Usually each player tunes to a single note played by the piano or oboe. The musicians make slight adjustments to string tension or pipe length whilst listening to the example note (frequency f_1) and the sound from their own instrument (frequency f_2). The aim of the adjustments is to get their instrument in exact unison with the example note ($f_1 = f_2$).

If the two notes are of slightly different frequencies then the player will hear this difference as a sort of wobble in the note. The loudness of the note will vary at the difference frequency ($f_1 - f_2$). The player would say the two notes are beating together, or that beats can be heard. ($f_1 - f_2$) is the **beat frequency**.

When two notes are of exactly the same frequency then no beats are heard, i.e. the beat frequency is zero.

Exploration 6.2

Apparatus:

◆ two signal generators ◆ two loudspeakers

This demonstration requires the same arrangement as Exploration 6.1 plus an extra signal generator, this time each loudspeaker is fed an independent waveform.

Feed one loudspeaker with a frequency of about 310 Hz and the other one with about 300 Hz, both at about the same loudness. Wherever you are in the lab, you will hear the two notes beating together at a beat frequency of about 10 Hz. If you then slowly change one of the signal generators so that the notes emitted by the loudspeakers approach unison you will hear the beat frequency getting lower and lower until it is inaudible.

There is a risk of damaging equipment from handling connectors and wires incorrectly when making connections to the signal generator, loudspeaker, etc. Follow the points below when undertaking this exploration.

1 Make sure all the equipment is switched off whilst setting up the circuit.

2 All connectors and the loudspeaker terminals must be insulated. Do not use bare connectors such as 'spade' connectors or crocodile clips.

3 Switch off before making any physical adjustments to the circuit.

20 MINUTES

It is also possible to 'see' the beat frequency if you set up the apparatus as shown in Figure 2.3(b) (Exploration 2.1) while you carry out this experiment.

The following questions are quite demanding, you are likely to need some help to answer them fully, accurately and efficiently. Ask a teacher for assistance or work with other students.

Assume the velocity of sound = 343 m s^{-1}.

Q2 Assume that a particular loudspeaker acts like an aperture with a diameter of 0.25 m. It is reproducing a sound tone with a frequency of 10 kHz. What is the approximate angular spread of the sound from the loudspeaker? Compare this with the value for 5 kHz and comment upon whether this is what you expected in terms of the relative wavelengths. ◆

Q3 Two loudspeakers, connected to the same signal generator, are producing the same 500 Hz tone. They are positioned 2 m apart. Draw a diagram showing how circular waves from each source superimpose, and calculate the positions of destructive and constructive interference. ◆

Q4 A loudspeaker producing a note of 1000 Hz is placed 2.3 m from a solid wall. What are the positions of loudest and quietest sound along the line between the speaker and the wall? ◆

Achievements

After working through this section you should be able to:

- describe the diffraction of a sound wave as it meets an obstacle and explain how the amount of spreading out that this causes depends on the size of the obstacle and also on the wavelength of the sound.

- describe how two sound waves can meet and interfere to produce either louder or quieter sounds

- describe how beats are made and what a beat frequency is.

Glossary

Beat frequency   The frequency of loudness variation as two similar frequency tones are heard simultaneously.

Beats   The effect heard when two similar frequency musical sounds are heard simultaneously.

Constructive interference   The combined effect of two equal wavelength waves meeting where the resulting displacement is larger than the displacements of the separate waves.

Destructive interference   The combined effect of two equal wavelength waves meeting where the resulting displacement is smaller than the displacements of the separate waves.

Diffraction   The spreading out of wave energy from holes or around obstacles that get in the path of the waves.

In phase   A description of moving systems where all elements move in the same direction at the same frequency at the same time (as in synchronized swimming).

Answers to Ready to Study test

R1

See Figure 6.5

R2

There would be constructive interference at A, because it is on the centre line and the paths from the two gaps are equal in length.

There would be destructive interference at B because the path difference is 1 cm, which is half the wavelength of the water waves.

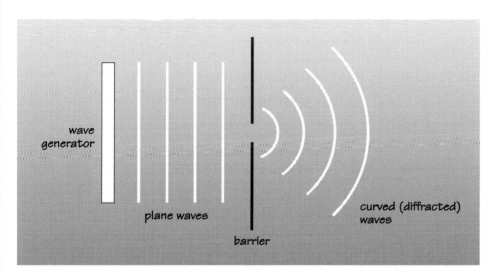

Figure 6.5
Plane wave fronts being diffracted by a gap in a barrier

Answers to questions in the text

Q1

Wavelength of the sound $= \dfrac{343\,\text{ms}^{-1}}{2000\,\text{Hz}}$

$$= 0.17\,\text{m}$$

Path difference $= 8.07\,\text{m} - 7.90\,\text{m}$

$$= 0.17\,\text{m}$$

i.e. one whole wavelength, so the two waves will meet in phase and you will hear a loud note.

Q2

$\text{Sin}\,\theta \approx \dfrac{\lambda}{D}$

so

$\theta \approx \sin^{-1}\left(\dfrac{\lambda}{D}\right)$

$v = f\lambda$

therefore

$\lambda = \dfrac{v}{f}$

$\lambda_1 = \dfrac{343\,\text{ms}^{-1}}{10 \times 10^3\,\text{Hz}}$

$$= 3.43 \times 10^{-2}\,\text{m}$$

$\theta_1 = \sin^{-1}\left(\dfrac{3.43 \times 10^{-2}}{0.25}\right)$

$$= 7.9°$$

$\lambda_2 = \dfrac{343\,\text{ms}^{-1}}{5 \times 10^3\,\text{Hz}}$

$$= 6.86 \times 10^{-2}\,\text{m}$$

$\theta_2 = \sin^{-1}\left(\dfrac{6.86 \times 10^{-2}}{0.25}\right)$

$$= 16°$$

The larger wavelength has the larger angular spread, i.e. the longer wave is diffracted more – this is expected.

Q3

$\lambda = \dfrac{v}{f}$

$ = \dfrac{343\,\text{ms}^{-1}}{500\,\text{Hz}}$

$ = 0.686\,\text{m}$

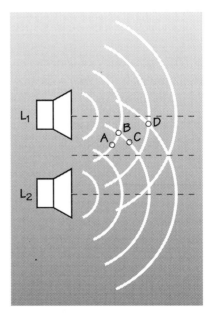

Figure 6.6 Points of constructive and destructive interference on wave fronts produced by two loudspeakers

Destructive interference at A and C.

Constructive interference at B and D.

$(\text{Length A to L}_2) - (\text{Length A to L}_1) = \dfrac{0.686}{2}\,\text{m}$

half a wavelength path difference, producing destructive interference.

(Length B to L_2) − (Length B to L_1) = 0.686 m

one whole wavelength path difference, producing constructive interference.

(Length C to L_2) − (Length C to L_1) = $\dfrac{0.686}{2}$ m

(Length D to L_2) − (Length D to L_1) = 0.686 m

There is constructive interference along the centre line because the distance to each speaker is equal, i.e. zero path difference.

Q4

$$\lambda = \frac{v}{f}$$

$$= \frac{343\,\text{ms}^{-1}}{1000\,\text{Hz}}$$

$$= 0.343\,\text{m}$$

The sound will be loud at the wall and at $\dfrac{0.343\,\text{m}}{2} = 0.171\,\text{m}$ intervals measured from the wall.

The sound will be quietest at positions halfway between the loud positions.

Many more people would like to hear a good concert than are lucky enough to be in the audience. Even the people there would probably like to enjoy the experience again. We take it for granted that we can buy recordings of the performances of successful bands and orchestras. It is even easy to record ourselves or our friends playing instruments and singing.

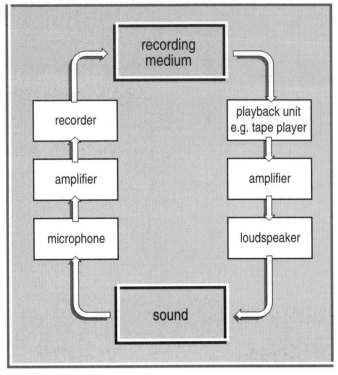

Figure 7.1
A complete (but simplified) sound recording and reproduction system

The left-hand side of Figure 7.1 shows how the sound at a concert can be recorded. Each block in the figure is essential for the information to be correctly stored on magnetic tape or compact disc. The right-hand side is the playback part of the system. This takes the stored information and converts it back into sound. If the whole system is working very well the sound produced by the playback part should be almost indistinguishable from the original concert, except quieter perhaps!

In the following sections of this unit we will examine how the blocks of this system work. We will also examine how magnetic tapes and compact discs work. We will start by considering how sound is picked up by a microphone and how it is produced by a loudspeaker.

When the sound of a concert is recorded, the sound itself isn't stored – it is converted to another form that can be stored.

The microphone and the loudspeaker in the sound recording and reproduction system are called **transducers**. Transducers convert signals from one form into another. Microphones convert sound into electricity and loudspeakers convert electricity into sound.

READY TO STUDY TEST

Before you begin this section you should be able to:

- recall and state the basic principles of electromagnetic induction from your GCSE course
- describe Fleming's rules for predicting direction of current flow through wires.

In the explorations in this section you will be connecting up sensitive electrical equipment. Before starting it you must make sure you are confident about connecting up this sort of apparatus – it is probably always best to get things checked by a teacher before switching anything on.

QUESTIONS

R1   Draw a simple circuit consisting of a lamp being supplied with electricity by a battery.

(a) Draw in an ammeter where it would measure the current flowing through the lamp.

(b) Draw in a voltmeter to measure the potential difference across the lamp.

(c) Add a resistor that would make the lamp dimmer.

(d) Add a switch that would switch off the electricity completely.

R2   What are the names of the poles of a magnet? How did they get them? Which is the direction of the magnetic field between the poles of a horseshoe magnet?

R3   Describe a way of making a magnetic field line pattern visible.

8.1 Microphones

The sound produced at a concert consists of pressure waves travelling through air from the musical instruments and the singers' vocal chords. The pressure changes are able to move light objects backwards and forwards, i.e. produce vibrations. This should be familiar to you from Section 3, but you may wish to look at that section again to refresh your memory. The pressure changes are very small, so things with a lot of mass will not be moved very much. A microphone must convert these small pressure changes into an electrical signal.

There are several types of microphone; each produces the electrical signal in a different way. One type is the **moving coil microphone**, which contains a very light coil of wire that vibrates in the field of a strong permanent magnet.

Electricity can be generated by moving a wire between the poles of a strong permanent magnet. This is called **electromagnetic induction**, and it is the principle behind the moving coil microphone. (Electromagnetic induction is covered more fully in the SLIPP unit on magnetic and gravitational fields.)

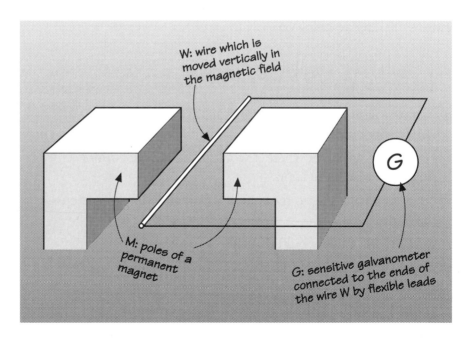

Figure 8.1   Producing electricity from movement

E **Exploration 8.1   Electromagnetic induction**

Apparatus:

◆ strong horseshoe magnet   ◆ lengths of wire   ◆ sensitive galvanometer
◆ plotting compass

Set up the equipment as shown in Figure 8.1.

Question 1 is based upon the experimental work you will carry out using this equipment. Make notes on what you discover, and leave the equipment set up in case you need to do more investigation.

Investigate the effects of:

■   changing the direction in which wire W is moved

■   rotating the magnet M so that its poles are reversed

■   moving the wire at different speeds in the magnetic field.

Q1   Refer to your notes on Exploration 8.1 to answer this question. If your notes are not adequate you can return to the equipment later to investigate further.

(a)   Draw a diagram to illustrate the relationship between the directions of the magnetic field (north pole to south pole), the generated current as it flows in the wire (it emerges from the end of the wire that has a positive voltage with respect to the other end) and the direction that the wire is moved through the magnetic field.

(b)   List the ways in which the generated electrical signal can be maximized, including ways that are not demonstrated in the experiment but nevertheless seem likely to you.   ◆

E **Exploration 8.2   Electromagnetic induction using a coil**

Apparatus:

◆ strong bar magnet   ◆ coils of insulated copper wire (with a range of numbers of turns)   ◆ several lengths of wire   ◆ sensitive galvanometer

A much larger electrical signal can be produced by using a coil and a bar magnet. Connect the ends of a coil with many turns to the galvanometer, probably one with a less sensitive scale than the one used in the previous exploration, and move the pole of a bar magnet towards and away from one end of the coil. Try coils with different numbers of turns. Does it matter whether you move the magnet or the coil?

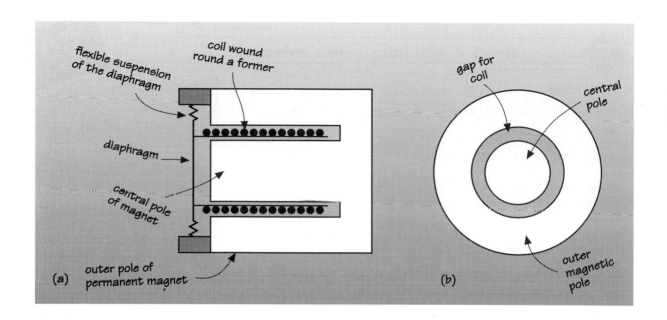

Figure 8.2
Cross-sections
through a moving
coil microphone:
(a) viewed from the
side, (b) viewed
from the end

How a microphone works

Electromagnetic induction is the principle behind the operation of moving coil microphones (and other devices, such as some pick-ups used to play vinyl discs).

The changing air pressure (the sound) causes the diaphragm to vibrate, which moves the coil in the magnetic field. A voltage is produced between the ends of the coil by electromagnetic induction; the voltage is called the **induced e.m.f.** The voltage will be changing in direction because the direction in which the coil moves is alternating.

Characteristics of a microphone

Microphones can be designed to have particular characteristics, e.g. to pick up sounds from only one direction or to pick up general background sound, but they must all be sensitive to the fairly small pressure changes caused by the sound source and to the full range of frequencies of sound produced at a concert.

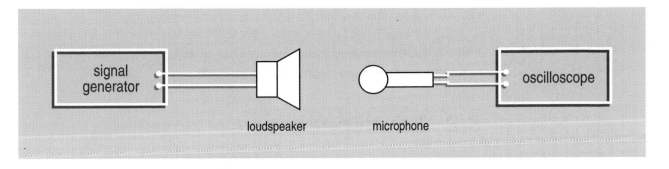

Figure 8.3   Comparing the response of a microphone with that of the human ear

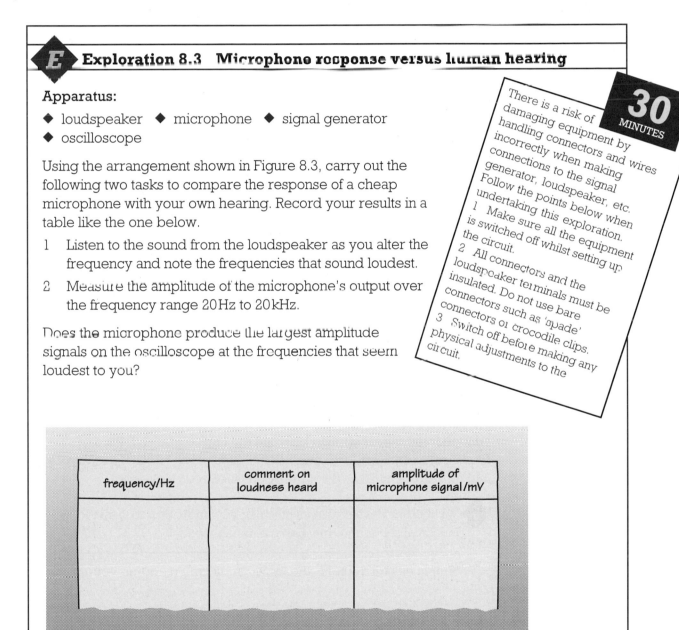

Exploration 8.3   Microphone response versus human hearing

Apparatus:

- loudspeaker ◆ microphone ◆ signal generator
- oscilloscope

Using the arrangement shown in Figure 8.3, carry out the following two tasks to compare the response of a cheap microphone with your own hearing. Record your results in a table like the one below.

1   Listen to the sound from the loudspeaker as you alter the frequency and note the frequencies that sound loudest.

2   Measure the amplitude of the microphone's output over the frequency range 20 Hz to 20 kHz.

Does the microphone produce the largest amplitude signals on the oscilloscope at the frequencies that seem loudest to you?

There is a risk of damaging equipment by handling connectors and wires incorrectly when making connections to the signal generator, loudspeaker, etc. Follow the points below when undertaking this exploration.

1   Make sure all the equipment is switched off whilst setting up the circuit.

2   All connectors and the loudspeaker terminals must be insulated. Do not use bare connectors such as 'spade' connectors or crocodile clips.

3   Switch off before making any physical adjustments to the circuit.

30 MINUTES

frequency/Hz	comment on loudness heard	amplitude of microphone signal/mV

Q2 Imagine that you are going to record a live performance, perhaps by a group of your friends who have formed a band or even a full orchestra. Discuss the advantages and disadvantages of using several microphones compared with using a single microphone. ◆

8.2 Loudspeakers

The construction of a loudspeaker is basically very similar to a moving coil microphone; both contain a movable coil and a magnet. In fact, a loudspeaker can be used as a microphone, but it will not be very sensitive.

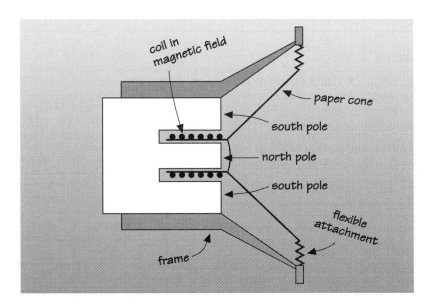

Figure 8.4
Construction of a loudspeaker

An electrical current is passed through the coil of the loudspeaker from an amplifier or a signal generator. The coil then experiences a force that tends either to push it out of the magnetic field or pull it in, depending upon the direction of the current. If an alternating voltage of a high enough frequency is applied between the ends of the coil, the loudspeaker will produce sound as the paper cone vibrates backwards and forwards, changing the air pressure slightly as it does so.

 What other devices use electromagnetic induction to convert an electrical signal into mechanical movement?

Simple electric motors, and moving coil ammeters and voltmeters.

Exploration 8.4   Sound production by loudspeakers

Apparatus:

◆ two loudspeakers – one large, one small   ◆ signal generator   ◆ strobe light

Observe the movement of the paper cone of a large loudspeaker connected to a signal generator. At low frequencies you can see the cone moving in and out, at higher frequencies the movement can be 'slowed' by observing the cone in flashing light from a stroboscope. Observe the cone over a wide range of frequencies. Can you tell from the amount of movement of the cone what range of frequencies the loudspeaker seems to be designed for? Is the range different for a small loudspeaker?

20 MINUTES

Strobe lights can cause epileptic fits in some people. Do not look directly into the flashing strobe light. Do not turn the frequency of the strobe below 20 Hz.

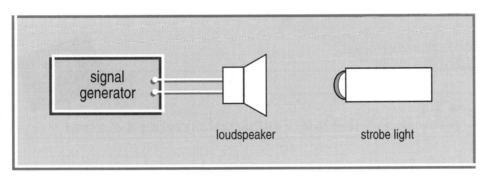

Figure 8.5 Arrangement of equipment for Exploration 8.4

Large loudspeakers in use at a rock concert

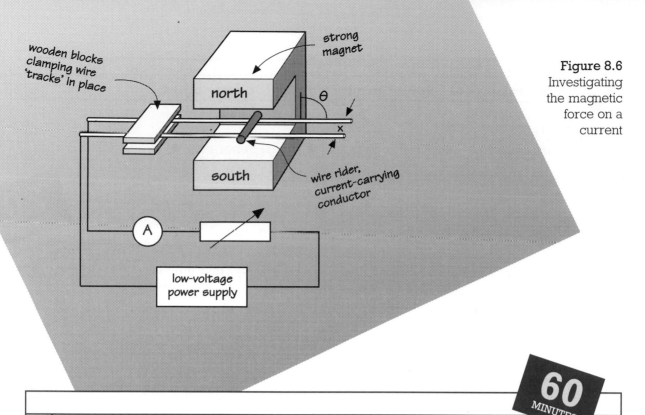

Figure 8.6
Investigating
the magnetic
force on a
current

60
MINUTES

Exploration 8.5
Magnetic force on an electrical conductor carrying a current

Apparatus:

◆ strong horseshoe magnet ◆ two long lengths and one short length of stiff copper wire ◆ two small wooden blocks ◆ small G clamp ◆ low-voltage power supply ◆ ammeter ◆ rheostat

There are a number of things that can be investigated with the set-up shown in Figure 8.6:

■ how the size of the force depends upon the current, I

■ how the size of the force depends upon the length of the conductor

■ the direction of the force for each current and magnetic field direction

■ the effect of changing the angle between the magnetic field and the current

■ the relationship between the directions of the magnetic field, the current and the force on the current.

Investigate each of these by changing I, x (the distance between the tracks) and θ. The force also depends upon the strength of the magnetic field: this is known as the **magnetic flux density**, B, which is measured in tesla (T). (Refer to your teacher or a standard textbook for a more rigorous investigation of the magnetic force on a current and Fleming's left-hand rule in particular.)

If the wire is perpendicular to the magnetic field the force on the wire, F, is given by the relationship:

$F = BIx$

where F is the force in newtons, B is the magnetic field strength in tesla, I is the current in amps and x is the length of the wire perpendicular to the magnetic field in metres.

Q3 Draw a diagram to illustrate the relationship between the directions of the magnetic field, the current and the force on the current. Refer back to your answer to Q1 and to your results for Exploration 8.5. ◆

 The Earth's magnetic field actually points roughly geographic south to geographic north. If a current flows from west to east in a wire, in which direction is the force on the wire due to the Earth's magnetic field?

Vertically upwards, as a correct answer to Q3 would have indicated.

Q4 If the separation of the wire tracks in Exploration 8.5 is 0.02 m, the rider is placed perpendicular to the tracks, the current is 0.50 A and the mass of the rider is 0.005 kg, what magnetic flux density is required to give the rider an acceleration of $10 \, \mathrm{ms^{-2}}$? ◆

Magnetic force on a coil

A coil placed in a magnetic field with a current flowing through it will generally experience a larger force than a straight wire, basically because the length of the conductor in the magnetic field can be greater. You will recall that a coil is more effective for electromagnetic induction too. This is why coils are used in both microphones and loudspeakers.

E Exploration 8.6   Making a basic loudspeaker

1-4 HOURS *this will vary according to the amount of preparation done beforehand*

Apparatus:

◆ thick cardboard ◆ stiff paper or card
◆ paper paste or masking tape ◆ scissors
◆ strong bar magnet ◆ 28 swg enamelled copper wire
◆ clamp stand ◆ signal generator

By following the instructions below and referring to Figure 8.7, make and test a simple loudspeaker. Change the number of turns in the coil of your loudspeaker and see what the effect is.

1   Start with a piece of thick cardboard.

2   Cut a circular hole in the centre (about 10 cm in diameter).

3   Cut out a circular piece of stiff paper with a diameter 3 or 4 cm more than the diameter of the hole.

4   Make a cut from the edge to the centre, this will be used to make an overlap to form a cone.

5   Cut small snips around the edge so that the rim of the cone can be splayed out to paste it to the edge of the hole.

6   Cut out a strip of paper large enough to make a tube that will just fit around the strong bar magnet without touching it.

7   Form the cylinder of paper and make snips around the edge of one end.

8   Splay out the snips at the end.

9   Stand the card so it is securely supported vertically. Make the cone and fix it to the card with glue.

10 Fix the cylinder to the point of the cone.

11 Take several metres of fine enamelled wire (about 28 swg) and form a tight coil around the paper tube, counting the number of turns. Connect the two ends of the coil to insulated 4 mm sockets for safe connection to the signal generator.

12 Clamp the bar magnet in a clamp stand so that it can be inserted into the open end of the paper coil former.

Make sure that the signal generator is switched off and connect the coil to it. Switch the signal generator on and carefully increase the output and adjust the frequency until some response is obtained. Investigate the effect of changing the number of turns on the coil (keep the same total length of enamelled wire by using it as the loose connecting wire to the signal generator sockets).

There is a risk of damaging equipment by handling connectors and wires incorrectly when making connections to the signal generator, loudspeaker, etc. Follow the points below when undertaking this exploration.

1 Make sure all the equipment is switched off whilst setting up the circuit.

2 All connectors and the loudspeaker terminals must be insulated. Do not use bare connectors such as 'spade' connectors or crocodile clips.

3 Switch off before making any physical adjustments to the circuit.

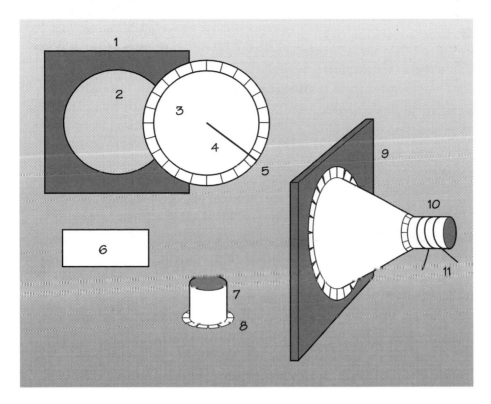

Figure 8.7 A home-made loudspeaker

Q5 Sketch a loudspeaker (clearly showing the direction of the magnetic field and the way the coil is wound on its former). Indicate which way the coil is moved by the magnetic force on a current flowing in a particular direction through it. ◆

The following questions are quite demanding, you are likely to need some help to answer them fully, accurately and efficiently. Ask a teacher for assistance or work with other students.

Q6 A loudspeaker has a coil with a diameter of 2 cm and 50 turns. It is placed in the field of a permanent magnet with a flux density of 0.4 T. What is the force on the coil if the current flowing through it is 100 mA? ◆

Q7 What happens if two flat coils are placed one on top of the other, and one is connected to an oscilloscope and the other to an alternating voltage power supply? Draw waveform graphs (voltage–time, flux density–time, etc.) to illustrate your answer. ◆

Achievements

After working through this section you should be able to:

- draw a block diagram of an audio system for the recording or reproduction of sound

- describe in detail the function and operation of microphones and loudspeakers

- construct a working loudspeaker

- apply knowledge of electromagnetic induction and the force on a current-carrying conductor in a magnetic field in new situations, including the relationship $F = BIx$

- apply Fleming's left-hand and right-hand rules.

Glossary

Electromagnetic induction   This is the phenomenon of electricity being generated when an electrical conductor is moved in a magnetic field. It is used in the design of some microphones (moving coil microphones) and dynamos.

Induced e.m.f.   When an electrical conductor is moved in the field of a magnet, electricity is generated (see *electromagnetic induction*). The voltage generated in this way is called the induced e.m.f. or electromotive force. Although it is a voltage, the historical terminology, which implies it is a force pushing the electricity, has been retained. It is much more common to refer to 'e.m.f.' than to 'electromotive force'.

Magnetic flux density (*B*)   Also called magnetic induction. Unit: tesla, T. This is a measure of the strength of a magnetic field. Magnetic fields are represented diagrammatically by lines; you can think of the magnetic flux density as the number of lines passing through unit area

perpendicular to the lines themselves. It does not take any account of the physical size of the magnet.

Moving coil microphone   One specific type of microphone. It is a transducer that converts sound signals into electrical signals. It consists of a coil inside a permanent magnet. Sound waves move the coil in the field of the magnet and this generates an electrical signal (voltage and current) by electromagnetic induction.

Transducer   A transducer converts signals or information from one form into another. As far as electronic systems are concerned, there are two types of transducer: input transducers, which convert various signals into electrical signals (e.g. microphones, light sensors, temperature sensors, position sensors, etc.), and output transducers, which convert electrical signals into other types of signal (e.g. loudspeakers, indicator lamps, moving coil meters, etc.).

Answers to Ready to Study test

R1

See Figure 8.8 – there are many correct variations, so check yours with a teacher if you are not certain whether you are right.

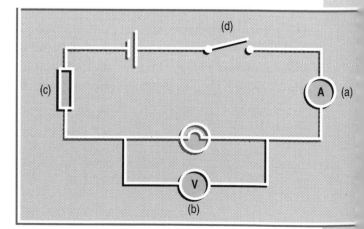

Figure 8.8

R2

The poles are called 'north' and 'south'. They got these names from the way a suspended bar magnet behaves – its north pole points north and its south pole points south! The direction of a horseshoe magnet's field is from its north pole towards its south pole.

R3

Magnetic field lines can be made visible in two ways:

1 Fine iron filings shaken on to a piece of paper placed in the magnetic field will tend to line up along the field lines. The piece of paper can be tapped gently to improve the pattern.

2 Plotting compasses, which are just miniature compasses, can be placed in the magnetic field. The magnetic needles will point along the field lines. The advantage of this method over iron filings is that the direction of the magnetic field can also be seen.

Answers to questions in the text

Q1

(a) The directions of the magnetic field, the current in the wire and the movement of the wire are commonly recalled using Fleming's right-hand rule (Figure 8.9). The thumb, first finger and second finger are held up so that each is at right angles to the others. The direction each points in represents one of the three quantities: thu**m**b for **m**ovement, **f**irst finger for **f**ield and se**c**ond finger for **c**urrent. Your diagram can be checked using this rule.

(b) The electric signal produced by electromagnetic induction can be increased in the following ways:

- moving the wire more quickly
- making sure the wire moves so that it is perpendicular to the magnetic field
- using a stronger magnet
- having a greater length of wire moving perpendicular to the field.

This can be shown by using a 'rectangular U-shaped' wire. The length of the bottom of the 'U' can be changed and moved at the same speed through the field. The longer it is, provided it does not stick out of the field, the larger the electrical signal will be.

Q2

A single microphone will pick up the nearest sounds best, its positioning would have to be carefully considered or some instruments might drown out the rest of the band or orchestra. However, only one 'track' of recording is taken with a single microphone, so a very simple recording device could be used. Using one microphone is simple and cheap, but the quality of the recording is likely to be poor.

Using several microphones results in several tracks of recording, some of which could, if necessary, be boosted by an amplifier so they are not lost under louder sounds. In other words, the separate tracks can be mixed to produce a better-quality result. The equipment needed would be much more complex and expensive, of course.

Q3

Fleming's left-hand rule is the way to remember this one (see Figure 8.10). The thumb now indicates the direction of the force or the **th**rust. The first and second fingers still

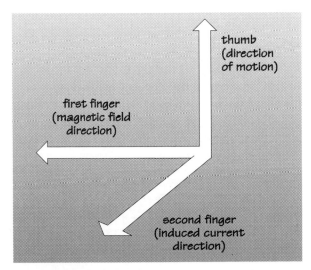

Figure 8.9
Fleming's right-hand rule

correspond to field and current respectively. (In the UK we drive on the *left* in our *motor* cars – this is how to remember that it is Fleming's *left*-hand rule for *motors* and *right* for dynamos).

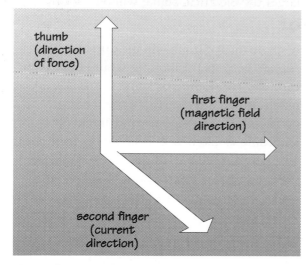

Figure 8.10 Fleming's left-hand rule

Q4

$$F = ma$$

$$B = \frac{F}{Ix}$$

$$= \frac{ma}{Ix}$$

$$= \frac{5 \times 10^{-3}\,\text{kg} \times 10\,\text{ms}^{-2}}{0.05\,\text{A} \times 0.02\,\text{m}}$$

$$= 5\,\text{T}$$

Q5

If the north pole of the permanent magnet is in the centre and the current is flowing anticlockwise, as viewed from the front of the loudspeaker, then the coil will be pulled into the gap between the poles of the magnet. All the other possibilities can be worked out from this.

Q6

$$F = BIx$$

x = number of turns × circumference of coil

$$= N \times 2\pi r$$

$$= 50 \times 2\pi \times (1 \times 10^{-2}\,\text{m})$$

therefore

$$F = 0.4\,\text{T} \times (100 \times 10^{-3})\,\text{A} \times 50 \times 2\pi \times (1 \times 10^{-2})\,\text{m}$$

$$= 0.126\,\text{N}$$

$$= 0.1\,\text{N (to one significant figure)}$$

Q7

If the coils are set up as in Figure 8.11, alternating current in coil 1 produces an alternating magnetic flux density. The alternating magnetic field induces an alternating e.m.f. in coil 2.

Induced e.m.f. in coil 2 is maximum when the magnetic flux density is changing most rapidly.

Your graphs should look something like those in Figure 8.12.

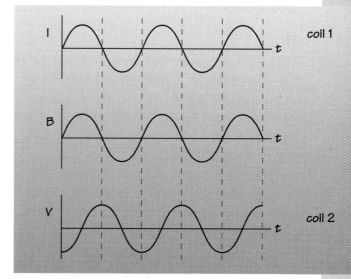

Figure 8.12 (above)

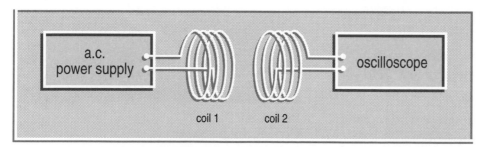

Figure 8.11

Both parts of a complete recording and playback system, illustrated by the block diagram in Figure 7.1, have amplifiers that are essential to their correct operation.

READY TO STUDY TEST

Before starting this section you should be able to:

■ use the relationship $V = IR$, and explain these terms: voltage or potential difference, V, current, I, and resistance, R

■ state the units of voltage, current and resistance

■ calculate electrical power from voltage and current values and know its units

■ explain the meaning of efficiency in terms of the energy transferred to a system and the energy transferred from a system (or in terms of the power supplied to a system and the power supplied by a system).

You must also be familiar with the use of logarithms (base 10), you should know:

■ $\lg (10^n) = n$

■ $\lg (10^m \times 10^n) = m + n$

QUESTIONS

R1 What is the resistance of a length of wire if 5 V must be applied between its ends to make the current flowing through it be 10 A?

R2 If a loudspeaker is 12% efficient and it is supplied with 20 W of electrical power, what is the power of the sound emitted from it? What happens to the rest of the power supplied to the loudspeaker?

R3 An amplifier supplies electrical energy at the rate of 10 W and with an average voltage of 2 V. What is the size of the average current flowing out of the amplifier?

R4 What are the logarithms (base 10) of the following?

(a)	100	(e)	1.0
(b)	62	(f)	0.25
(c)	10	(g)	0.1
(d)	3.2	(h)	0.02

9.1 The functions of amplifiers

An amplifier is an electronic device that processes an electrical signal. Generally speaking, it makes the signal bigger by increasing the electrical power, so either the voltage or the current, or both, are increased. Making the signal larger ensures that it does not get lost in any noise that is picked up, such as mains hum or noise generated in the electronic circuits themselves. There may be situations where a smaller electrical signal is needed; an amplifier can still be used but its **gain** will be less than 1:

$$\text{gain (as a function of some variable)} = \frac{\text{output value of the variable}}{\text{input value of the variable}}$$

The most commonly used type of gain is **voltage gain**, in which case the output signal parameter is the output voltage and the input signal parameter is the input voltage. However, an amplifier can also have **current gain** or **power gain**, in which cases the parameters are current and power respectively.

If a gain is greater than 1 the output is larger than the input, if the gain is less than 1 then the output has been made smaller by the amplifier.

The amplifier has to process the electrical signal in a number of ways, so it might well consist of several separate amplifiers, each of which carry out a particular function (see Figure 9.1).

Recording amplifier

The **equalizer** is an amplifier that is matched to the particular type of microphone being used (or to a pick-up on a musical instrument such as a guitar). It makes sure that the signal

```
signal from
microphone
    ↓
 equalizer
    ↓
gain control
    ↓
bass control
    ↓
treble control
    ↓
power amplifier
    ↓
signal to
recording device
```

Figure 9.1
A recording
amplifier

A good quality hi-fi
system

going to the next stage is the same whatever the source of the signal. This is because different transducers produce different amplitude signals and are more sensitive at different frequencies. The equalizer effectively standardizes the signal fed to the next stage. It will have a fixed gain or a switchable gain, so it can be used for several different input devices.

The **gain control** amplifier has variable gain – it changes the signal level – so it is basically a volume control.

The **bass control** and **treble control** modify the **tone** of the signal – both have a variable gain. Musical information is spread over more than one frequency; the bass control will boost (or reduce) frequencies within the signal that are below approximately 1 kHz, and the treble control will boost (or reduce) the higher frequencies.

The **power amplifier** makes sure that the signal going to the recording device has sufficient electrical power to produce a change on the recording medium. This stage will have a fixed gain.

Playback amplifier

This is similar to the recording amplifier. It has an equalizer that is matched to the player (e.g. a tape deck or CD player) being used. The gain control amplifier provides volume control. Then there are the tone controls. Finally, the power amplifier ensures that there is sufficient electrical power to drive the loudspeaker.

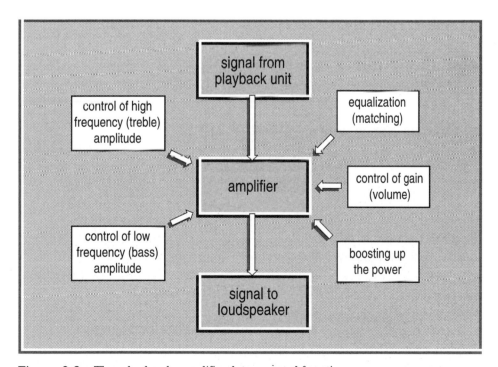

Figure 9.2 The playback amplifier has several functions

9.2 Characteristics of a 'black box' amplifier

The important features of an amplifier are its gain and how it behaves at different frequencies. These are most easily summarized by graphs that show how the gain depends upon the frequency of the signal being fed into the amplifier. Generally these graphs have a logarithmic horizontal scale for the frequency and a linear vertical scale for the gain in **decibels** (dB). (Effectively the vertical scale is also logarithmic because the number of decibels is related to the logarithm of the power or voltage ratio.)

$$\text{power gain in dB} = 10 \lg\left(\frac{\text{power out}}{\text{power in}}\right)$$

$$= 10 \lg\left(\frac{P_o}{P_i}\right)$$

as power $\propto$ voltage squared or $P \propto V^2$

$$\text{voltage gain in dB} = 10 \lg\left(\frac{V_o^2}{V_i^2}\right)$$

$$= 20 \lg\left(\frac{V_o}{V_i}\right)$$

[*Note:* lg denotes logarithm base 10 (common logarithm). Do not confuse this with ln, which is the logarithm base e (natural logarithm).]

 An amplifier has a voltage gain of 150, i.e. $\frac{V_o}{V_i} = 150$. What is this in decibels?

$$\text{Voltage gain in decibels} = 20 \lg\left(\frac{V_o}{V_i}\right)$$

$$= 43.5\,\text{dB}$$

The use of decibels is particularly appropriate to describe **audio amplifiers** because of a property of human hearing. In order to be able to hear both very quiet sounds and very loud ones, perception by the human brain is not proportional to sound intensity. A sound that we think is twice as loud as another sound does not have twice the intensity. The loudest tolerable sound the human ear can hear has an intensity 10^{12} times the quietest that can be heard (the **threshold of hearing**). The decibel scale more closely resembles the response of the ear. A whisper is about 30 dB above the threshold of hearing and normal conversation is about 60 dB above the threshold of hearing – normal speech sounds about twice as loud as whispers, but the intensity of the sound of a normal voice is about 1000 times that of a whisper, as the following calculation shows:

if

$$\text{power out} = 1000 \times \text{power in}$$

$$\text{power gain} = 10 \lg\left(\frac{1000P}{P}\right)$$

$$= 10 \lg(1000)$$

$$= 10 \times 3\,\text{dB}$$

$$= 30\ \text{dB}$$

Then any increase of 30 dB is equivalent to a thousand-fold increase in power.

Using the same equations will show you that a change of 20 dB is equivalent to a simple ratio power gain of 10^2 and a change of 40 dB is equivalent to a simple ratio of 10^4

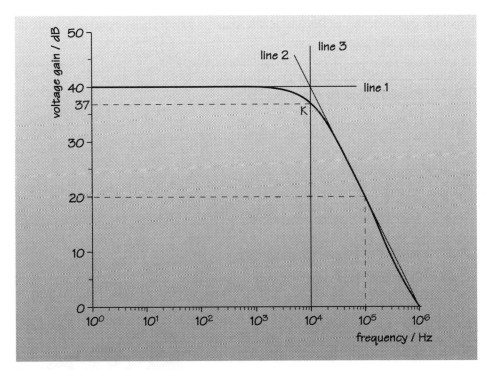

Figure 9.3
Frequency response curve of a DC amplifier

Figure 9.3 describes how a DC amplifier treats signals of different frequencies – a DC amplifier will amplify frequencies as low as 0 Hz, i.e. DC. The vertical scale shows voltage gain in decibels. A change of 20 dB is equivalent to a change in the simple ratio voltage gain of 10, e.g. the voltage gain at 1 Hz (10^0 Hz on the horizontal axis) is 40 dB or 100 as a simple ratio. At 10^5 Hz or 100 kHz the voltage gain is 20 dB, which is a ratio gain of just 10. Refer back to the equation for the voltage gain to clarify this for yourself.

A similar amplifier to the one in the previous question has a voltage gain of 1500. What is this gain when it is expressed in decibels?

$$\text{Voltage gain in decibels} = 20 \lg\left(\frac{V_o}{V_i}\right)$$

$$= 63.5\,\text{dB}$$

Notice that the curve has a long horizontal flat part; this means that signals of all frequencies up to the 'knee' (K) of the curve are equally amplified. The range of frequencies for which the amplifier has a **flat response** is known as the **bandwidth** of the amplifier; because it is a DC amplifier the 'width' is measured from 0 Hz to the frequency at the 'knee'.

The straight lines 1, 2 and 3 are construction lines to find the bandwidth of the amplifier. Lines 1 and 2 are drawn first, following the two almost straight parts of the frequency response curve. Where lines 1 and 2 cross a third line is drawn vertically. Line 3 shows that the bandwidth of the amplifier is 10^4 Hz or 10 kHz. This covers most of the audible range so it would be useful as an audio amplifier. Line 3 crosses the frequency response curve at the point where the gain is 37 dB, in general it is 3 dB less than the 'flat gain'.

 Exploration 9.1   Properties of an amplifier

Apparatus:

- ◆ black box amplifier   ◆ signal generator
- ◆ dual low-voltage power supply (+/0/−)
- ◆ dual trace oscilloscope

We have called the amplifier used for this investigation a 'black box' because it is not important, at least at this stage, to know how *all* of its parts work. It will be used to discover general ideas of *how it behaves*, which will apply to most amplifiers.

There is a risk of damaging equipment by handling connectors and wires incorrectly when making connections to the signal generator, loudspeaker, etc. Follow the points below when undertaking this exploration.

1 Make sure all the equipment is switched off whilst setting up the circuit.

2 All connectors and the loudspeaker terminals must be insulated. Do not use bare connectors such as 'spade' connectors or crocodile clips.

3 Switch off before making any physical adjustments to the circuit.

60-120 MINUTES

At the heart of the amplifier there is an **integrated circuit** (an operational amplifier) that determines the absolute maximum gain of the amplifier circuit; this is about 100 dB or ratio voltage gain of 100000. This is too high for this investigation because all input signals would have to have amplitudes less than about 0.1 mV. The maximum voltage gain can easily be reduced by changing the value of one resistor in the circuit. The resistor values for maximum voltage gains of 1000 (60 dB), 100 (40 dB), 10 (20 dB) and 1 (0 dB) are 10 MΩ, 1 MΩ, 100 kΩ and 10 kΩ respectively. Some instructions should accompany the circuit to tell you which resistor to change and to identify the connections to the circuit.

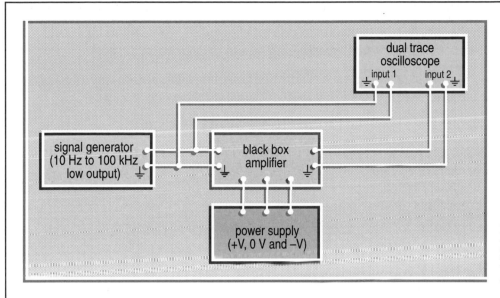

Figure 9.4
Investigating the
bandwidth of an
amplifier

Connect up the black box amplifier to the power supply, the signal generator and the dual trace oscilloscope as in Figure 9.4.

The power supply must provide positive and negative voltage in addition to zero voltage because the output of the amplifier will alternate between positive and negative voltage just as the input from the signal generator does and draws on its power supply to do so.

The signal generator is used to feed small-amplitude sinusoidal voltages into the amplifier. If the voltage amplitude is too large the amplifier will 'saturate' (which means it cannot amplify the signal without distorting it), so be careful to keep the amplitude low – a square wave output for a sine wave input is a sign of saturation. The frequency will be set to several values in the range 10 Hz to 100 kHz and the gain will be calculated at each of these; the gain will change if the frequency is above the bandwidth of the amplifier. Start with the amplitude set very low.

A dual trace oscilloscope is used so that the output from the amplifier can be compared with the signal being fed into it from the signal generator. The oscilloscope input (input 1) used to monitor the signal generator will need to be set to a sensitive volts per division range. The input used for the amplifier output (input 2) will be on a much less sensitive range for the higher maximum gains.

Start with the amplifier set up for a maximum gain of 1000 (60 dB), the signal generator set to 100 Hz and the oscilloscope timebase set to 2 ms per division.

With everything switched on you should see two traces on the oscilloscope if the signal generator output is above zero and the oscilloscope sensitivity settings are appropriate. Once you have everything working at this frequency you can start collecting data in a table like the one overleaf.

When you have increased the frequency so that you have reached the 'knee' of the frequency response curve you will need to plot more points to see the detailed shape of the graph.

Notice what effect the amplifier has upon the phase difference between the input and the output, i.e. their relative horizontal positioning on the oscilloscope screen.

Change the value of the resistor to give a different maximum gain. Repeat the readings. Plot the frequency response curves so that they are similar to the one in Figure 9.3.

What is the bandwidth of the amplifier for each maximum gain setting?

If possible, leave this apparatus set up so you can hear the effect of limited bandwidth in a poor amplifier as discussed later.

max. gain/dB	frequency/Hz	input amplitude/V	output amplitude/V	gain ratio	gain/dB
60	100				
60	10				
60	1,000				
60	5,000				
60	10,000				
etc.					

 What is the overall gain of two amplifiers connected in series if each has a voltage gain of 10 (20 dB)?

100 (40 dB), because the first amplifies the voltage of the signal by a factor of 10 and the second amplifies by 10 again. Note that we multiply the two gain ratios or add the two dB values.

 If the two amplifiers each had a bandwidth of 10 kHz, what would be the bandwidth of the two-stage amplifier?

Just less than 10 kHz, because the knee of each amplifier's frequency response is at 10 kHz where the gain of each amplifier is slightly less than 20 dB. Just below 10 kHz the gain of the combination will be flat at 40 dB.

Q1 The bandwidth of an amplifier is greater at lower gain settings. For example, if a typical black box amplifier is set to a voltage gain of 60 dB or 1000 it has a bandwidth of only 1 Hz. This bandwidth is too small for a system that is processing the frequencies in human speech, never mind the higher frequencies in music. How could gains of 60 dB or higher be achieved with bandwidths of 10 kHz or more? ◆

9.3 Amplifiers and human hearing

Poor amplifiers

It is important that audio amplifier systems are able to amplify all the frequencies in a signal that people can hear. You can hear the effect of a poor amplifier by using the black box amplifier with the maximum gain set to 60 dB.

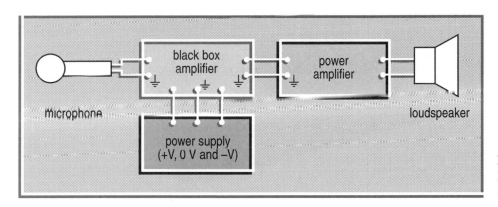

Figure 9.5
Hearing the effect of a poor amplifier

The moving coil microphone can be used to detect speech, singing, the notes from a musical instrument or music from a hi-fi system loudspeaker. You can hear the result of processing by a poor amplifier (such as your experimental version) in headphones driven by a power amplifier. (The power amplifier provides volume control and enough power for the headphones.) The outputs of the microphone and of the amplifier can also be displayed on an oscilloscope. Try this for the other maximum gain settings of the black box amplifier. Can you hear the effect of limited bandwidth?

Stereophonic sound

Some animals, such as dogs, are able to detect the direction of a sound source because they hear the sound in both ears. If a dog turns its head towards the sound until both ears hear it equally loudly, then its nose will be pointing at the sound. People can do the same thing – in fact we are able to tell where a sound is coming from without turning our heads partly because of the different level of loudness in each ear. Hearing music in stereo increases our appreciation of it, we get a sense of the relative positions of the instruments and singers, it makes the music more interesting and often special effects are used to give us the impression of movement.

Dogs make full use of stereo hearing

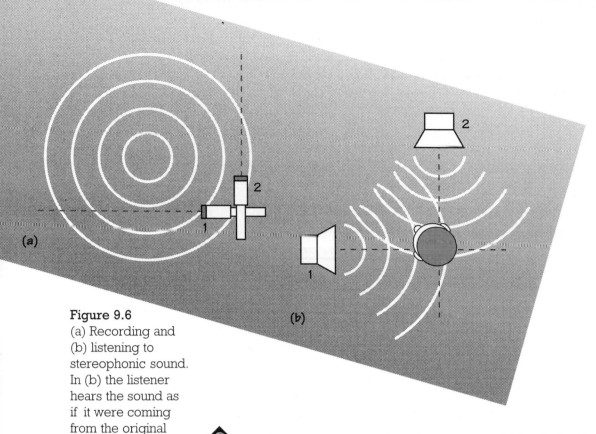

Figure 9.6
(a) Recording and
(b) listening to
stereophonic sound.
In (b) the listener
hears the sound as
if it were coming
from the original
source and would
need to turn slightly
to the left to face the
imaginary source

To what extent is reproduced stereo sound like the real sound that was recorded?

It is actually very different, but we get the impression that it is very similar as a result of careful recording and correct positioning of the loudspeakers coupled with adjustment of the balance control. So it is different but it is perceived to be similar.

Two directional microphones are used to detect the sound, effectively dividing it into two directional components, as shown in Figure 9.6(a). The signals produced contain information on the phase and loudness of the sound as it is arrives at each microphone. Microphone 1, which is most nearly facing the sound source, will produce the biggest signal.

The sound is reproduced by two loudspeakers. If these are placed at 90°, as the microphones were, imagine trying to face the apparent source of the sound. The loudspeaker on the left-hand side of Figure 9.6(b) will produce the louder sound because the corresponding microphone detected more sound, so you will turn so that your right ear is facing more towards the upper loudspeaker. You will be facing in the general direction of an imaginary sound source somewhere between the loudspeakers.

Exploration 9.2   Using stereophonic hearing

60-120 MINUTES

If any equipment is brought in from home for this exploration it should be given a full safety check by a competent person before use.

Apparatus:

◆ stereo tape deck to play and record ◆ pair of microphones
◆ headphones ◆ blank tape

1   Make a recording to test someone's ability to use their stereophonic hearing. Place a chair in a fixed position and arrange the microphones in the approximate positions of the ears of someone sitting in the chair. Then make sounds in different places around the room while recording, noting the position and sequence of the sounds.

2   Play back the recording through headphones to a series of people sitting in the chair. Make sure they face in the right direction and don't turn their heads at any time in the course of the test. Ask them to point in the direction from which the sound appears to come and note the response as an angle or in terms of a clock face (straight ahead as 12 o'clock, 90° to the right as 3 o'clock, and so on).

 Recordings of concerts are often made using several microphones. The explanation of stereo sound above considered only two microphones. How is the stereo effect produced if a lot of individual microphones are used for the separate instruments and vocalists involved in a live concert?

The left and right channels finally recorded on to the magnetic tape or CD are mixed from all the separate channels corresponding to each microphone, pick-up, etc., in use during the concert. The mixing is a skilled job as it can affect the quality of the final recording so much. Some instruments might be predominantly on one track, one vocalists might be placed on the right track and another on the left, and so on. Listen to some recordings to see if you can hear how individual parts have been placed on the stereo channels (you might find this easier with recordings of classical music).

The following questions are quite demanding, you are likely to need some help to answer them fully, accurately and efficiently. Ask a teacher for assistance or work with other students.

Q2   An amplifier with an input resistance of $10\,k\Omega$ receives the signal which has an amplitude of $10\,mV$ from a microphone. The amplifier feeds a loudspeaker (resistance $8\,\Omega$) a signal with an amplitude of $5\,V$. What are the voltage, current and power gains as ratios? ◆

Q3   If an amplifier has a bandwidth of $1.0\,Hz$ when its gain is $100\,dB$, and $100\,Hz$ when its gain is $60\,dB$, what gain should it be set to in order to achieve a bandwidth of $1000\,Hz$? ◆

Achievements

After working through this section you should be able to:

- explain the need for amplification in audio systems

- define gain (voltage, current and power)

- describe different functions of amplifiers in audio systems

- express power and voltage gain as ratios or in decibels and convert between the two ways of expressing gain

- understand the term 'intensity' when applied to sound

- explain what is meant by 'threshold of hearing'

- explain and use the terms 'frequency response' and 'bandwidth' as applied to amplifiers

- use signal generators and oscilloscopes to investigate the frequency response of an amplifier

- describe a good audio amplifier in terms of its flat frequency response and adequate bandwidth

- explain that high-gain, good audio amplification is achieved using multi-stage amplifiers

- recall that general purpose and audio amplifiers are available as integrated circuits

- give the reason for stereo hearing in animals and humans

- describe how stereophonic information is stored in recordings and how the effect is reproduced

- appreciate that a commercial recording is mixed from many individual sound tracks

Glossary

Audio amplifier An amplifier is an electronic device that increases the size of an electrical signal. The signal size can be measured in terms of voltage, current or power, so amplifiers are often categorized as voltage, current or power amplifiers. An audio amplifier is used for frequencies that are audible when in the form of sound, i.e. in the range 20–20 000 Hz, approximately. This frequency range is called its bandwidth. The amount by which the amplifier increases the size of the electrical signal is expressed by its *gain*. The gain of an amplifier should be approximately constant throughout the bandwidth. (See *flat response*.)

Bandwidth The range of frequencies for which an amplifier has a flat response, i.e. its gain remains constant with frequency. For an audio amplifier this should cover all the frequencies within the audible frequency range of sound that is of interest: 100–3400 Hz, approximately, for speech only or 20–20 000 Hz for hi-fi music.

Bass control Audio amplifiers generally have variable gain, which is adjusted by the gain control and changes the amplitude of all the frequencies in the same proportion. To change different frequencies by different amounts the amplifier needs tone controls. The bass control adjusts the amplitude of the signal components with frequencies typically below about 1 kHz. (See *treble control*.)

Current gain Current gain equals output current divided by input current. (See *gain*.)

Decibel (dB) A unit of comparison of two power levels, e.g. two electrical powers or two sound powers. It is obtained from the simple ratio of the powers, P_2/P_1, as follows:

$$\text{comparison in decibels} = 10 \lg\left(\frac{P_2}{P_1}\right)$$

A comparison in decibels involves the logarithmic function, so each factor of ten increase in power results in an increase of 10 dB in the comparison. Comparisons in decibels are more meaningful than simple ratios for sound because of the way our ears respond to sound power. (See *threshold of hearing*.)

Equalizer   A special type of amplifier that corrects for characteristics of particular input transducers of an audio system. For example, an audio amplifier might be designed to take electrical signals from a tape deck, a CD player and a microphone. Each of these may have a different effect upon basically the same audio information so each needs some compensation for its particular effect. Perhaps the microphone produces a larger amplitude electrical signal when it detects high-frequency sound than when it detects a low-frequency sound, even though the actual sounds had the same amplitude. The reverse might be the case for the tape deck. Clearly the same input to the amplifier cannot be used for both of these, so each has its own input that leads into its own equalizer. Each equalizer output is the same for the same audio information.

Flat response   The way in which amplifiers deal with different frequencies can be shown using graphs of gain against frequency. These are called frequency response curves. Audio amplifiers in particular have constant gain for a range of frequencies (the audible frequencies of sound), so the curve is a horizontal, straight line, i.e. a flat line. In this region the amplifier is said to have a flat response, which is good if it covers the correct frequency range.

Gain   The ratio by which an amplifier increases the size of an electrical signal is expressed as its gain. (See *audio amplifier*.) A number of variables can be used to describe the size of an electrical signal, in particular voltage, current and power, so the gain can be the voltage, current or power gain. In each case the gain is the ratio of the size of the variable at the amplifier's output to its size at the input. Gain equals output variable divided by input variable.

Gain control   Amplifiers often have variable gain. For example, the position of the spindle of a variable resistor is altered to adjust the gain; this variable resistor is the gain control.

Integrated circuit (IC)   A complete circuit manufactured as a single small component. The individual components and interconnections are microscopic in size and produced on a single chip of silicon as patterns of particular impurities and metallization. The chip is enclosed in a package, usually of black plastic, and connections are made via metal pins set into the packaging. Common ICs are rectangular with 4, 7 or 8 pins along each of the longer sides. ICs range from very simple (e.g. individual logic gates) to very complex (e.g. powerful microprocessors).

Power amplifier   An electronic device that increases the power of an electrical signal. The amount by which the power is increased is given by the power gain. A power amplifier is the final stage of an audio system before the loudspeaker or the recording device. It ensures that the electrical signal being converted into sound or stored in some form is able to operate the output transducer.

Power gain   Power gain equals output power divided by input power. (See *gain*.)

Threshold of hearing   The minimum sound power at a particular frequency that produces a response, i.e. that can be heard. It is used as the comparison power level when sound levels are specified in decibels. The threshold of hearing power is P_1 in the expression $10 \lg(P_1/P_2)$, which is used to calculate decibel sound levels.

Tone Music, speech, etc., contain a mixture of different frequencies with different amplitudes. The tone is a quality of sound ranging from 'trebly' when high frequencies have largest amplitude to 'bassy' when low frequencies are loudest. The tone of the sound reproduced by an audio system can be changed using a treble control and a bass control. A pure tone means a single frequency note.

Treble control The treble control adjusts the amplitudes of the signal components with frequencies typically above about 1 kHz. (See *bass control*.)

Voltage gain Voltage gain equals output voltage divided by input voltage. (See *gain*.)

Answers to Ready to Study test

R1

$$R = \frac{V}{I}$$

$$= \frac{5.0\,\text{V}}{10\,\text{A}}$$

$$= 0.5\,\Omega$$

R2

If 12% of the electrical energy is used to produce sound, then

$$\text{sound power} = \frac{12}{100} \times 20\,\text{W}$$

$$= 2.4\,\text{W}$$

The remaining 88% of the energy supplied to the loudspeaker is transferred through heating the loudspeaker and its surroundings.

R3

Electrical power $P = V \times I$

so

$$I = \frac{P}{V}$$

$$= \frac{10\,\text{W}}{2\,\text{V}}$$

$$= 5\,\text{A}$$

R4

(a) 2.00

(b) 1.79

(c) 1.00

(d) 0.51

(e) 0.00

(f) −0.60

(g) −1.00

(h) −1.70

Answers to questions in the text

Q1

Several stages of amplification can be used. A 'black box' amplifier with a maximum gain of 20 dB, or 10, has a bandwidth of about 100 kHz. Using two 20 dB stages gives a total gain of 40 dB, or 100, three stages gives 60 dB, and so on, but the bandwidth is still well over 10 kHz.

Q2

$$\text{Voltage gain} = \frac{\text{Output voltage}}{\text{Input voltage}}$$

$$= \frac{5\,\text{V}}{10 \times 10^{-3}\,\text{V}}$$

$$= 5 \times 10^2$$

$$\text{Current} = \frac{\text{voltage}}{\text{resistance}}$$

therefore

$$\text{output current} = \frac{5}{8}\,\text{A}$$

$$= 0.625\,\text{A}$$

and

$$\text{input current} = \frac{10 \times 10^{-3}}{10 \times 10^3}\,\text{A}$$

$$= 1 \times 10^{-6}\,\text{A}$$

so

$$\text{current gain} = \frac{0.625\,\text{A}}{1 \times 10^{-6}\,\text{A}}$$

$$= 6.25 \times 10^5$$

Power = voltage × current

therefore

$$\text{power gain} = \text{voltage gain} \times \text{current gain}$$

$$= 500 \times 6.25 \times 10^5$$

$$= 3 \times 10^8 \text{ (to one significant figure)}$$

Q3

See Figure 9.7. Gain should be set to 40 dB to achieve a bandwidth of 1000 Hz.

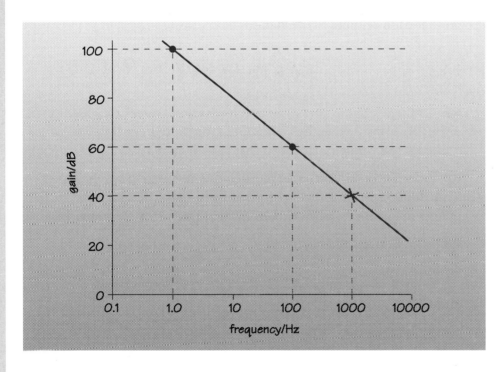

Figure 9.7

The most important ways of distributing recordings of music are on magnetic tape cassettes and on compact discs. Both have their advantages and disadvantages and they are very different in several ways that are interesting in terms of the physics and technology involved.

In this section you will use the expressions:

$$v = f\lambda$$

relating wave velocity to frequency and wavelength;

$$v = \frac{s}{t}$$

for velocity in terms of displacement and time taken; and

$$F = ma$$

describing the relationship between force, mass and acceleration.

These should be very familiar to you and are used in the questions that follow. You will also use binary numbers, so it is a good idea to remind yourself about them now.

QUESTIONS

R1   If the magnetic tape in an audio-cassette moves at a speed of 4.75×10^{-2} m s^{-1} when it is recording, how long must the tape be to record the whole of a concert that lasts 45 minutes?

R2   If the frictional force that must be overcome to move the tape in an audio-cassette is 1 N, with what force must the tape be pulled so that it moves at a constant speed of 4.75×10^{-2} m s^{-1}?

R3   (a) Convert the binary numbers 111, 1010 and 110011 into decimal.

(b) Convert the decimal numbers 8, 15 and 47 into binary numbers.

10.1 Magnetic tape

Magnetic recording of sound has been around throughout the twentieth century. Gradually it has progressed and become better and simpler. Today we think nothing of making our own recordings and playing commercially produced ones.

Recording on to magnetic tape

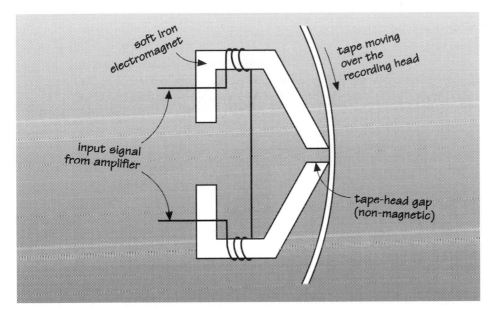

Figure 10.1
The tape recording head

Figure 10.1 shows the recording head of a tape recorder. A plastic tape coated with magnetic material such as iron or chromium oxide is run past the head at a controlled speed. The magnetic material is **magnetized** and the amount by which it is magnetized is roughly proportional to the size of the electrical signal fed to the recording head by the amplifier. As the electrical signal alternates between positive and negative voltages, the magnetization will also alternate between north and south.

If the frequency of the signal is f and the speed of the tape is v, the magnetization on the tape will have a wavelength λ. This is the length of one cycle of magnetization corresponding to one cycle of the electrical signal:

$$\lambda = \frac{v}{f}$$

You came across this relationship as $v = f\lambda$ in Section 2.4.

The wavelength of the magnetization on the tape becomes important when the recording is replayed – it affects the maximum frequency that can be played and determines the size of the **tape-head gap** and the tape speed.

Reproducing an electrical signal from a recording on tape

The tape runs past a replay head, which is identical to the record head except that now an electrical signal is induced in the coils as the magnetic field of the tape passes the gap.

 What principle is being used here?

Electromagnetic induction.

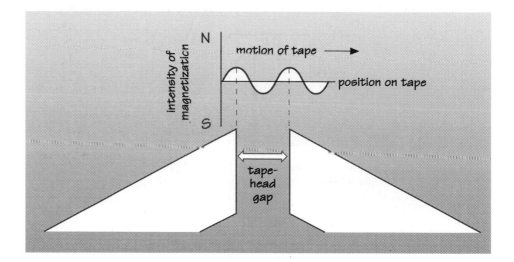

Figure 10.2
The signal picked up by the replay head

In Figure 10.2 the wavelength of the magnetization on the tape is equal to the size of the tape-head gap. This means that the magnetization is always the same at the two edges of the gap. If the magnetization is the same at both edges no signal is induced in the coils of the replay head. In contrast, if the wavelength is double the tape-head gap then the magnetization at the two edges will be completely out of step and the total magnetisation within the gap will change between maximum north, zero and maximum south. All wavelengths between these two result in reduced response by the replay head.

So, the maximum frequency that you require to record and play back should produce a magnetization wavelength on the tape that is twice the tape-head gap.

Q1 The normal velocity of the tape in a cassette player is $4.75 \times 10^{-2} \text{ms}^{-1}$. If the maximum frequency that can be recorded is 15.0kHz, what is the size of the tape-head gap, g? ◆

Q2 Recording studios have machines that can record frequencies up to 24kHz. If one of these machines has a tape-head gap of 4.0 μm, calculate the velocity at which the tape must run. ◆

Machines that use magnetic tape

There is an enormous variety of audio machines that use magnetic tape in one form or another. They range from recording studio machines that can record many tracks simultaneously or separately, to tiny pocket dictation machines. Magnetic tape is also used to make **digital** recordings now. Compact discs store information digitally, so the principles behind digital recordings will be dealt with in the next section. Videotapes are also magnetic tapes, of course – they store visual (video) information as well as a sound track.

10.2 Compact discs

Compact discs (CDs) are made of plastic with a reflective metal coating, which is itself coated with plastic to protect it. A 12 cm diameter CD can hold 74 minutes of recorded sound. The sound is stored digitally as billions of tiny pits in the plastic. Playing a CD does not produce noise like playing a vinyl disc or a magnetic tape, and CDs do not wear out and become distorted in normal use. This is because the sound is digitized and also because there is no physical contact between the player and the surface of the disc.

Digitization of analogue signals

The electrical signal produced by a microphone is **analogue** – it can vary *continuously* between maximum positive and negative voltages. The information stored on a CD consists of a sequence of 16 binary digits or a 16 'bit' number, i.e. every piece of information is one of 32768 different codes. Digital information is not continuous like analogue information, it has a limited number of possible values – 32768 in this case.

To digitize the information in an analogue voltage signal, samples of the voltage have to be taken at regular intervals. Each of these samples is then converted into the binary code that most closely matches the value of the voltage. (See Figure 10.3.)

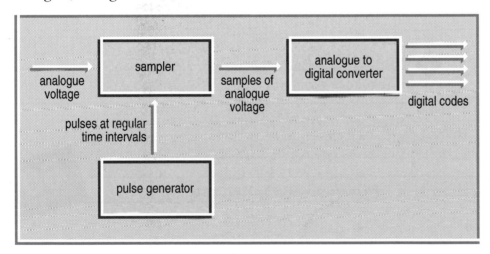

Figure 10.3
Sampling and converting analogue voltages into digital codes

Sampling the analogue signal

The voltage samples are like snapshots of the voltage as it changes with time, or like the frames in a film of continuous action. So, for good quality digital sound, we need the right number of 'snapshots' per second. This can be illustrated graphically as shown in Figure 10.4 overleaf – the analogue voltage and its samples are shown on the same time axis. Sixteen samples have been taken during each complete cycle of the alternating voltage in this instance.

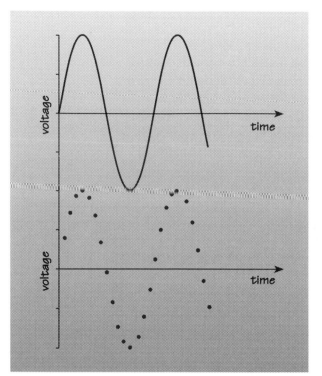

Figure 10.4
Analogue voltage
signal and samples

As the shape of the analogue voltage can be clearly seen from the sample positions, 16 samples per cycle are obviously enough. Twenty-four frames per second are enough for a movie, unless of course something is moving very fast. You may have seen films in which a wagon's wheels appear to be going slowly backwards when the wagon is moving forwards at high speed.

? What is the absolute minimum number of samples per cycle of an analogue waveform?

Two. Carry out the following exploration to see why.

E ▶ **Exploration 10.1   Minimum sampling rate**

60 MINUTES

Apparatus: ◆ graph paper ◆ pencil

Draw a roughly sinusoidal function with about four complete cycles at the top of a piece of graph paper.

Underneath, using the same time axis, plot samples of the waveform taken at regular intervals for the cases when 8, 4, 2 and 1.5 samples are taken per cycle (avoid the zero-crossing points as places when you take the samples).

You should have five mini-graphs, one below the other, all using the same time scale.

You will see that information about the original shape is lost as the number of samples is reduced. With less than two samples per cycle even information about the frequency is lost.

You can reach the same conclusion by an experimental investigation, which will give you more practice at using an oscilloscope.

E **Exploration 10.2** **The effect of sampling at a low frequency**

Apparatus:
- the sampler circuit   ◆ signal generator
- dual trace oscilloscope   ◆ dual low-voltage power supply

Set up the arrangement in Figure 10.5 using the 'sampler' circuit prepared for you and the instructions for connecting it to the power supply, signal generator and oscilloscope.

Set the signal generator (the *analogue* signal source) to 100 Hz with an amplitude of 1 V; this should be found on one of the traces of the dual trace oscilloscope. The sampler contains a pulse generator with a frequency of about 2 kHz. Adjust the oscilloscope so that you have the second trace showing the samples, about 20 samples per cycle. The samples should accurately reflect the shape and frequency of the analogue signal.

Increase the frequency of the analogue voltage in stages, observing how well it is represented by the samples at each stage.

There is a risk of damaging equipment by handling connectors and wires incorrectly when making connections to the signal generator, loudspeaker, etc. Follow the points below when undertaking this exploration.
1 Make sure all the equipment is switched off whilst setting up the circuit.
2 All connectors and the loudspeaker terminals must be insulated. Do not use bare connectors such as 'spade' connectors or crocodile clips.
3 Switch off before making any physical adjustments to the circuit.

60-120 MINUTES

The information provided by the samples as you reach an analogue voltage frequency of about 1 kHz should hardly indicate what the analogue waveform really is; above 1 kHz the samples should give the impression that the analogue signal has a lower frequency than it actually does. This shift to lower frequency is called **aliasing distortion** – the reproduced signal would have more bass than the original signal.

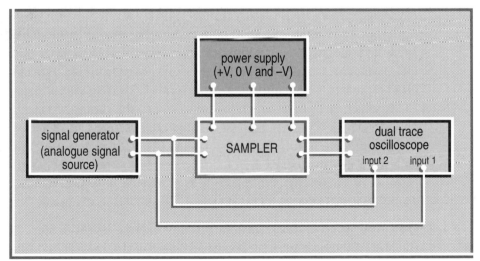

Figure 10.5
Investigation of signal sampling

A 10 kHz note is sampled at the minimum frequency that avoids aliasing distortion and converted into 8-bit codes. The codes are sent one bit at a time down a wire. What is the bit-rate down the wire?

---

160 000 bits per second. The minimum allowed sampling frequency is 20 kHz (twice 10 kHz), so there will be 20 000 samples every second. Each sample is converted into 8 bits, so there will be $8 \times 20\,000 = 160\,000$ bits every second.

Q3   During the recording of a master CD, 44 100 samples are taken of the audio signal every second. Each sample is converted into a 16-bit code.

(a) What is the theoretical maximum signal frequency that can be successfully reproduced from the information stored on the CD?

(b) If a CD has 74 minutes of *stereo* music recorded on it, how many binary digits does the whole disc have on it, excluding any that are there to indicate where tracks start and end? ◆

Analogue-to-digital converters and digital-to-analogue converters

The samples of the analogue voltage, all 44 100 of them every second, are converted into 16-bit codes by an integrated circuit called, quite obviously, an **analogue-to-digital converter**. These devices are actually very common and were around long before CDs – they are used in digital voltmeters, thermometers and many other digital devices.

When a CD is played, the binary codes are read from the protected surface; these have to be converted back into analogue voltages. This is done by another integrated circuit, the **digital-to-analogue converter**. The player then interpolates between the voltage values of adjacent samples to reproduce an almost smooth waveform again, which can then be amplified and fed to loudspeakers.

A voltage cannot be precisely represented by a binary code when it undergoes analogue-to-digital conversion. For example, imagine that a sinusoidal electrical signal with an amplitude of 2.5 V is to be converted into a sequence of 4-bit codes. The codes range from 0000 to 1111. Let 0000 represent −2.5 V and 1111 represent +2.5 V. The count from 0000 to 1111, which is 15 in decimal, is equivalent to the difference between −2.5 V and +2.5 V, i.e. 5 V. The smallest voltage change that can be registered in the binary form is 1/15, or 6.67%, of 5 V. (This fraction or percentage is called the **resolution**.) Obviously the resolution gets better (smaller) if the number of binary digits in the code is increased, it is just 0.00152% for a 16-bit code (1111 1111 1111 1111 is 2^{15} or 32 768 in decimal).

Q4   The 16-bit codes represent discrete voltage levels or steps. What is the size of the voltage step as a percentage of the maximum voltage that could be recorded? (In other words, what is the resolution?) ◆

Compact disc technology

To make a CD, a master has to be cut first. The blank master CD spins at a high speed and the digital information controls a powerful laser. The laser's beam cuts pits into the metal of the disc. This disc is then used to stamp an impression into softened plastic discs. The stamped plastic discs are then plated with aluminium and coated with protective clear plastic.

A CD player

When a CD is being played, a low-power laser beam follows the spiral track of pits from the centre towards the edge of the disc. The pits in the disc break the reflected laser beam into pulses of light. The light pulses are converted into electrical pulses by a light sensor.

If you look at the playing surface of a CD through a microscope you can just about see the pattern of pits as small dots.

CD-ROM

CDs have other applications besides storing music. Particularly important is the CD-ROM. One disc can hold 250 000 pages of text, which is more than enough for all of the words in *Encyclopedia Britannica*. Information stored on CD-ROM can include photographs, animated sequences and sound as well as text, all of which can be accessed using a computer.

Q5 Compact discs have many advantages over magnetic tape cassettes. These are:

- absence of background noise
- no deterioration of the recording due to wear
- no moving parts to damage
- tracks can be played in any order
- wider dynamic range (the difference between the quietest and the loudest sound that can be recorded).

Can you think of any advantages that magnetic tape cassettes have over CDs? ◆

Q6 Using your answer to Q3(b) estimate the area and diameter of the region taken up by one bit on the surface of a disc. (Remember a compact disc is 12 cm in diameter.) ◆

Achievements

After working through this section you should be able to:

- explain the differences between *analogue* and *digital* recordings

- state that recordings on magnetic tape can be analogue or digital, and that commercially available recordings on tape have mainly been analogue

- state that recordings on compact discs are digital

- describe the processes involved in recording an electrical signal on to magnetic tape

- describe the processes involved in reproducing an electrical signal from a recording on magnetic tape

- carry out calculations involving the relationships between tape speed, signal frequency and tape-head gap

- describe the sampling of an analogue signal that is the first stage of converting it into digital form

- calculate the minimum sampling rate for a particular signal and describe aliasing distortion

- investigate the effect of sampling at different frequencies using a sampler circuit, a signal generator and an oscilloscope

- explain the term 'analogue-to-digital conversion'

- carry out calculations involving code length in bits, bit rate and sampling frequency

- explain the term 'digital-to-analogue conversion'

- describe how information is stored on a compact disc and read off it using laser light

- list the relative advantages of CDs and magnetic tapes.

Glossary

Aliasing distortion   Part of the process of analogue-to-digital conversion is sampling the analogue signal. If time between samples is too long (i.e. the sampling frequency is too low) the digital codes will not accurately represent the original analogue signal. It will have a lower frequency than the original (an alias). This type of distortion is avoided by using a sampling frequency that is at least twice the highest frequency in the analogue signal.

Analogue   Signals can be analogue or digital. Analogue signals can have any value between limits, e.g. an analogue voltage can have any size between 0 V and 5 V, say. In contrast, a digital voltage can have only certain discrete values.

Analogue-to-digital converter (ADC)   An electronic device that converts an analogue voltage, which can be continually varying, into a sequence of binary codes representing the analogue voltage at instants in time. An ADC has two major parts: a sampler and the ADC proper. The sampler takes samples of the analogue voltage at regular intervals and the ADC proper converts each sample into a binary code.

Digital   Signals can be analogue or digital. Digital signals can only have certain specific values, e.g. 0 V or 5 V say. In contrast an analogue voltage can have any value between limits. During analogue-to-digital conversion a voltage of any value is converted into a binary number that is equivalent to the nearest digital voltage – the intervals between adjacent binary numbers can be likened to a step in the equivalent voltage.

Digital-to-analogue converter (DAC)   An electronic device that converts a binary code into an analogue voltage.

Magnetization Magnetic tape is coated with material that can permanently hold magnetism. A blank tape has no net magnetism. The process of giving the material its magnetism is called magnetization. However, the degree or polarity to which it is magnetized can also be called the magnetization, e.g. strongly magnctized could be referred to as high magnetization and being given a north pole as north magnetization.

Resolution The size of the voltage step as a percentage of the maximum voltage that can be recorded.

Tape-head gap The recording and playback heads of a tape recorder/player are like horseshoe electromagnets. The gap between the 'poles' of the horseshoe is the tape-head gap.

Answers to Ready to Study test

R1

Number of seconds in 45 minutes

$$= 45 \times 60\,s$$
$$= 2700\,s$$

Length of tape needed

$$= 2700\,s \times 4.75 \times 10^{-2}\,m\,s^{-1}$$
$$= 128.25\,m$$
$$= 128\,m \text{ (to three significant figures)}$$

(*Note*: quoting the answer to three significant figures would be correct as this is consistent with the least accurately quoted measurement: $4.75 \times 10^{-2}\,m\,s^{-1}$. However, if in practice you were to use this length of tape you would not record 45 minutes' worth of sound.)

R2

If the tape is to move at constant speed it must have a total force acting upon it that is zero, as a net positive force would result in an acceleration. Therefore the driving force must be just sufficient to overcome the frictional force, i.e. $1\,N$.

R3

(a) 111(binary) is equivalent to
$$1 + 2 + 4 = 7 \text{ (decimal)}$$
1010 (binary) is equivalent to
$$2 + 8 = 10 \text{ (decimal)}$$
110011 (binary) is equivalent to
$$1 + 2 + 16 + 32 = 51 \text{ (decimal)}.$$

(b) 8 (decimal) is equivalent to 1000 (binary)
15 (decimal) is equivalent to 1111 (binary)
47 (decimal) is equivalent to 101111 (binary).

Answers to questions in the text

Q1

$$g = \frac{\lambda}{2}$$
$$= \frac{v}{2f}$$
$$= \frac{4.75 \times 10^{-2}\,m\,s^{-1}}{2 \times 15.0\,kHz}$$
$$= 1.58 \times 10^{-6}\,m$$
$$= 1.58\,\mu m$$

Q2

$$v = f\lambda$$
$$= 2fg$$
$$= 2 \times 24\,kHz \times 4.0\,\mu m$$
$$= 0.19\,m\,s^{-1} \text{ or } 19\,cm\,s^{-1}$$

Q3

(a) Maximum signal frequency

$$= 0.5 \times \text{sampling frequency}$$

$$= 22\,050\,\text{Hz}$$

(b) Number of bits per channel

$$= \text{number of bits per sample}$$
$$\times \text{sampling frequency} \times \text{playing time}$$
$$= 16 \times 44\,100\,\text{s}^{-1} \times /4 \times 60\,\text{s}$$
$$= 3.13 \times 10^9$$
$$= 3.1 \times 10^9 \text{ (to two significant figures)}$$

For stereo (two channels) the total number is doubled, i.e. 6.27×10^9.

Q4

$$\text{Resolution} = \frac{1}{2^{15}} \times 100\%$$

$$= \frac{1}{32768} \times 100\%$$

$$= 3.05 \times 10^{-3}\%$$

Q5

Advantages of magnetic tape:

- the tape can be erased and reused
- people can make their own recordings
- individuals can choose what tracks to record on to a blank tape
- tape players are cheaper than CD players
- tapes have been around longer so there is a greater variety of old recordings available on tape
- tapes are relatively inexpensive
- more generally than compact cassettes, master recordings on magnetic tape can be cut and spliced, removing unwanted sections of recordings.

Q6

The radius of a CD is 6.0 cm

$$\text{Area per bit } A \approx \frac{\text{disc area}}{\text{number of bits per disc}}$$

$$= \frac{\pi r^2}{N}$$

$$= \frac{\pi \times (0.060\,\text{m})^2}{3.13 \times 10^9 \times 2}$$

$$= 1.8 \times 10^{-12}\,\text{m}^2$$

$$\text{Diameter of a bit} \approx \sqrt{A}$$

$$= 1.34 \times 10^{-6}\,\text{m}$$

$$= 1.3\,\mu\text{m}$$

(to two significant figures).

(*Note:* Both of these results are overestimates, some of the disc area is not used for recording bits – there is a hole in the centre surrounded by a space and the edge of the disc is also blank.)

11.1 Recording a concert

A concert is frequently recorded with many microphones, but the CD that is eventually sold has just two tracks – left and right.

Summarize the whole process involved from making the recording using microphones at the concert to playing the recording back through loudspeakers at home by talking it through with another student, or making a list of bullet points of essential features.

11.2 Reproduction of music in a disco

DJs in discos still prefer to use vinyl discs so that they can mix tracks from the recordings of different groups, this way they can create particular moods. A good DJ is very skilled at setting up each successive track to blend in with the one before. Cassette tapes are not suitable for this because the tape has to be run from one reel to the other until the desired track is found.

A DJ sets the mood at a disco

Theoretically, CDs could be used for mixing in discos – some equipment is already being manufactured for this. Eventually the skill will probably have gone out of DJing, to a large extent, as the technology takes over.

Try to draw a block diagram of an audio system that could be used in a disco. Remember that two tracks have to be blended into one another to avoid periods of silence that break the mood of the people dancing.

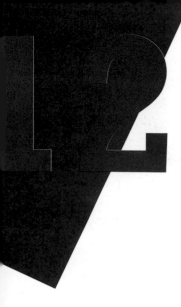

12.1 Introduction

When you are listening to a performance in a concert hall you expect to hear the music free from any distortion or interference. These could be internal echoes, outside noise, vibrations in the hall and the loss of certain frequencies by absorption. To achieve this the entire structure of the hall must be carefully designed on paper before the JCBs arrive at the site.

The Symphony Hall at the City of Birmingham International Convention Centre needed to be one of the best concert halls in the world. The site found for it was crossed by a railway, canals and busy roads, which produced a lot of noise and vibration (see Figure 12.1).

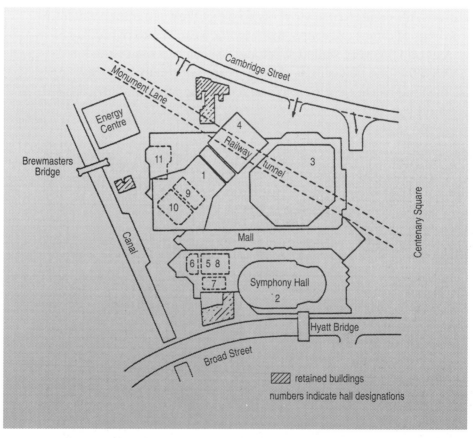

Figure 12.1   The site of the Symphony Hall

The best current design and construction techniques were used to overcome these problems so that the Symphony Hall could be built in an ideal location for access by the public.

The first stage of the design was to eliminate low-frequency vibrations carried through the ground from a railway tunnel that was already on the site. A special isolated railway track had to be installed and the whole building, which includes two convention halls as well as the Symphony Hall, was to be supported on deep, heavy piles (see Figure 12.2). Figure 12.3 shows the effect of the special rail track before and after installation.

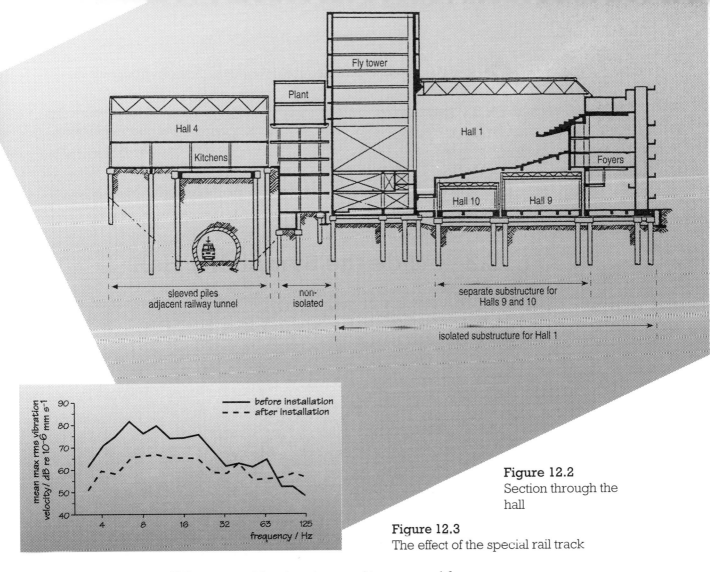

Figure 12.2

Section through the
hall

Figure 12.3

The effect of the special rail track

The Symphony Hall itself floats on rubber bearings and is separated from
the rest of the building by special jointing systems (Figure 12.4) which
eliminate lateral vibrations.

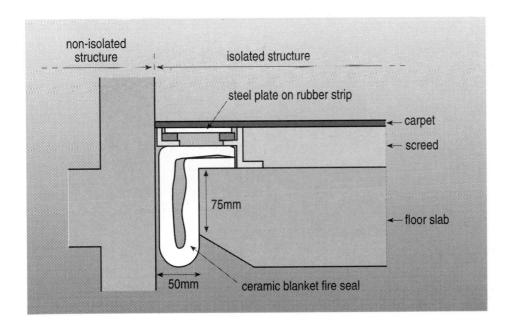

Figure 12.4

Anti-vibration joint

How does a rubber strip reduce unwanted vibrations from outside the hall?

It absorbs the energy of the vibrations because of its non-rigid form and heats up as a result.

The Symphony Hall has been acclaimed by performers and critics alike for its superb acoustic performance.

12.2 Inside the Symphony Hall

There are several features of the internal design of the hall that affect its **acoustics**. These are

- volume of the auditorium
- reverberation chambers
- canopy
- balconies
- seats
- curtains
- entrance/exit lobbies
- wall panels.

Inside the Symphony Hall

Large halls are needed for the loud sound produced by large, powerful orchestras or highly amplified rock groups. Also, to raise enough money to pay for the performers, the hall must have a lot of seats to accommodate a large audience. Large halls may tend to have long reverberation times (which means that the sound continues to **reverberate** for a long time after it is produced): the larger the hall, the longer the reverberations. In a poorly designed hall this will be worse when there is no audience – the people act like acoustic absorbers. Other acoustic absorbers, such as curtains and soft wall panels, are included in the designs of good halls so that reverberations are reduced to acceptable levels even during rehearsals. The bottoms of the seats are good reflectors of sound, but they are positioned at an angle so that they reflect as much sound down to the absorbing floor as a person would absorb if they were sitting in the seat.

 What properties of a material make it a good sound absorber? Suggest some suitable real materials.

Good sound absorbers are likely to be soft, flexible, low density, rough or foamy. Suitable materials are expanded polystyrene, cottonwool, glass fibre and fibreboard.

To achieve particular effects the acoustics of the hall can be changed. For example, the hall can be made to sound like a cathedral by turning some sound absorbing wall panels so that they become reflectors. These increase the reverberation times, which makes the hall 'echoey' like a cathedral. This effect can be emphasized by moving the reflective canopy above the stage vertically upwards. The volume of the auditorium can also be increased by opening up reverberation chambers on either side of the stage. These chambers are very 'echoey' because of their hard walls and they can also be tuned to different frequencies. Alternatively, the hall can be made as acoustically dead as a recording studio, so that there are no echoes. This effect is produced by closing the reverberation chambers and using all the absorbing wall panels.

The impact, clarity and strength of the sound from the stage that reaches the back of an audience is dramatically improved by reflective, oblique surfaces on the side walls beneath the balconies. Soft sounds that would be lost in a poorly designed hall are heard by everyone thanks to this design feature.

 What properties of a material make it a good sound reflector? Suggest some suitable real materials.

Good sound reflectors are likely to be hard, rigid, high density, smooth or solid. Suitable materials are concrete, steel and hard woods.

Sound coming from outside the hall would be very distracting to an audience or a live performer, so the entrances are designed to prevent sound getting into the auditorium.

 How can you prevent sound entering the auditorium through an open door?

Give the lobby a right-angle bend and make the walls from sound-absorbing material.

12.3 Quantifying the acoustics of a hall

Effective gain of the hall

Without any reflective surfaces near to a sound source the intensity of the sound falls off inversely with the square of the distance from the source for sources radiating equally in all directions:

$$I = \frac{k}{d^2}$$

where I is the sound intensity reaching a receiver at a distance d from the source and k is a constant.

In a hall, because of reflection, the intensity received at a particular point is greater. So, from the point of view of a listener, the hall effectively has a gain compared with an open space; this can be expressed as a simple ratio or in decibels. (You met gain and decibels earlier in Section 9.)

If the intensity received at a distance d in the open air is I_o, and the intensity received at the same distance inside a hall is I_i, then the effective gain of the hall, G, is given by:

$$G = \frac{I_i}{I_o}$$

or

$$G = 10 \lg \frac{I_i}{I_o}$$

in decibels.

Reverberation time of the hall

A simplified way of measuring a hall's reverberation time is to produce a sound and time how long it takes it to become inaudible. This time depends upon your position in the hall as well as the features of the hall.

The pin-drop test

A pin dropping on to a smooth wooden surface produces a small sound. You can measure the clarity of the hall's acoustics by finding the largest distance at which this sound is audible.

◆ PROJECT ◆

QUANTIFYING THE ACOUSTICS OF A REAL HALL

Apparatus:

- ◆ pin ◆ smooth piece of wood ◆ tape measure
- ◆ long mains extension lead ◆ power breaker safety plug
- ◆ loudspeaker ◆ signal generator ◆ microphone
- ◆ amplifier for microphone (may be useful) ◆ oscilloscope

The purpose of this project is to make measurements of some acoustic properties of a real hall. The tasks can be split between different people and the results pooled, or it can be done as a more substantial project. If several people do it as a project based upon different halls, then the quantitative data and qualitative features of each hall can be compared.

Task 1: Effective gain of the hall

60 MINUTES plus analysis

You will require an open space, preferably a field near to your school or college building. Hard ground is not good because it will reflect sound. You need to measure the sound intensity travelling a certain distance inside the hall you are testing and the same distance in the open space. Only the location is different, everything else must be the same (same equipment, same settings, etc.)

There is a risk of damaging equipment by handling connectors and wires incorre when making connections to th signal generator, loudspeaker, etc. Follow the points below when undertaking this exploration.

1 Make sure all the equipment is switched off whilst setting up the circuit.

2 All connectors and the loudspeaker terminals must be insulated. Do not use bare connectors such as 'spade' connectors or crocodile clips.

3 Switch off before making any physical adjustments to the circuit.

Only attempt the outdoor task on a dry day. The mains extension lead should be connected via a power breaker plug or a socket protected by a residual current device.

Set up the equipment outside, as shown in Figure 12.5. The microphone, amplifier and oscilloscope part of the arrangement need to be placed at a distance d away from the rest. You can use several different values for d, but start with the largest value you are going to use. Adjust the signal generator to 1.0 kHz and turn the amplitude up until it is quite loud. The microphone will detect the sound and the oscilloscope can be used to measure the amplitude of the amplified signal. Set the controls of the amplifier and the

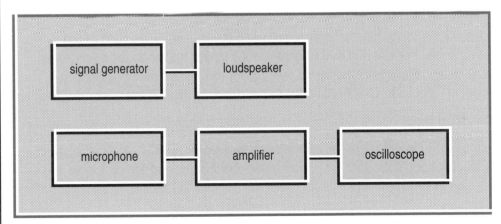

Figure 12.5 Measuring effective gain of a hall

oscilloscope so that the amplitude can be measured easily and accurately. The amplitude of the signal is a voltage that we will call V_O. The intensity of the sound is proportional to this voltage squared. Record all the data in a table like the one shown below.

Without adjusting any of the settings on the signal generator, the amplifier or the oscilloscope, move the equipment into the hall.

distance, d/metres	V_O/volts	V_O^2/volts^2	V_i/volts	V_i^2/volts^2

Repeat the whole experiment inside the hall; you will be measuring V_i now, which you should record in the table.

You can then calculate the effective gain of the hall for each distance, either as a fraction or in decibels.

$$G = \frac{I_i}{I_o} = \frac{V_i^2}{V_o^2}$$

or

$$G = 10 \lg \frac{I_i}{I_o} = 10 \lg \frac{V_i^2}{V_o^2} = 20 \lg \frac{V_i}{V_o}$$

in decibels

Task 2: Reverberation time of the hall

A signal generator and loudspeaker are used to carry out this investigation. Set them up in the same way as for the first task in a certain position in the hall. For this experiment you need a pulse of sound. To make a pulse, pull one of the loudspeaker plugs out of the signal generator socket and then produce the sound pulse by rapidly pushing it into the socket and immediately pulling it out again. You are likely to hear this sound sustained as a series of echoes, especially if all the curtains are open and the hall is empty. Time how long the sound is sustained for – this is a measure of the reverberation time. Repeat this in different places in the hall and under different conditions, e.g. try closing the curtains, setting out the chairs and bringing in a large group of people. You can also repeat the experiment using different sound frequencies.

Task 3: Pin-drop test

Drop a pin from a fixed height on to a smooth, horizontal piece of wood placed on the stage or at one end of the hall. Then measure the distance at which the sound becomes just inaudible.

If you are able to repeat this experiment in several other halls you can compare the acoustic properties of your hall with that of other halls and discover how different features are associated with good or bad acoustics

Achievements

By the end of this section you should be able to describe features that affect the acoustic properties of a room.

Glossary

Acoustics   The scientific study of sound wave production, propagation and properties. Also used loosely to refer to the properties of a room that determine how a sound is transmitted and heard in that room.

Reverberate   The continuation of sound transmission as if in a series of echoes.

If you think back to the beginning of this unit, you will realize what a long way you have come – from your first exploration, which involved blowing over the tops of milk bottles or twanging rubber bands, through making a loudspeaker, to considering how to design a concert hall to produce the best acoustic properties!

To help you to appreciate how far you have come, look back through the list of achievements for each section. If you feel unsure about any of them, go over the relevant section(s) of this unit again. When you feel fairly confident about most of these achievements ask your teacher for the exit test for this unit. When you have done the test, consult your teacher, who has the answers and will probably wish to go through them with you. We hope you have enjoyed learning about sound, music, recording and reproduction with this supported learning unit, and that you want to use more units in the series.

CONCLUSION

Acknowledgements

Grateful acknowledgement is made to the following sources for permission to reproduce material in this unit.

Photographs and figures

p. 7: Jazz Band – Dat's Jazz Picture Library; p. 47: Tocoma Narrows bridge – photographic collection, Tocoma Public Library, USA; p. 50: Nigel Kennedy – Hulton Deutsch Picture Library; p. 77: Clarinet – Mike Levers, The Open University; Trumpet – Boosey & Hawkes Musical Instruments Limited; p. 85: Water wave diffraction – Coastal Energy Research Centre, US Department of the Army; p. 86: Louis Armstrong – Hulton Deutsch Picture Library; p. 94: Concert – International Convention Centre; p. 101: Loudspeakers – Robert Ellis, REPFOTO; p. 110: Hi-fi system – Philips Consumer Electronics; p. 131: CD player – Philips Consumer Electronics; *Encyclopedia Britannica* – Mike Levers, The Open University; p. 135: DJ – Joe Giron, REPFOTO; pp. 136–7: Figures 12.1–12.4 – Ove Arup & Partners; p. 138: Interior of Symphony Hall – International Convention Centre.

Index

absorption 139

acoustics 138, 141, 143

adiabatic 76, 80

air columns 23, 51–5, 57–9
   see also pipes

air resistance 26, 30

aliasing distortion 129–30, 132

amplifiers 94, 109–122
   audio 112, 114, 117 , 120
   bandwidth 114–16, 120
   black box 112–16
   DC 113
   equalizer 110–11, 121
   gain control 110, 111, 121
   playback 111
   power 110, 111, 121
   recording 110–11

amplitude 10, 11, 13, 14, 21

analogue 127, 132

analogue-to-digital converter 127, 130, 132

anti-phase 19–20, 84

antinode 63, 68

Armstrong, Louis 86

atmospheric pressure 24

audio amplifier 112, 114, 117 120

auditory nerves 24

bandwidth 114–16, 120

Barton's pendulums 30–1, 32

bass control 110, 111, 120

beat frequency 89, 91

beats 89, 91

binary code 127, 130

Birmingham International Convention Centre 136

black box amplifier 112–16

bulk modulus 75, 78, 80

cassette tapes 135

CD-ROM 131

CDs *see* compact discs

chromium oxide 125

circuit noise 110

clamped reed vibrations 51

closed pipes 52, 68

coils 103

compact discs 94, 119, 127–31, 135
   player 131
   see also CD-ROM

compass, plotting 97, 107

compression 33, 37, 55, 56, 60

concerts
   see also halls
     hall design 136–40
     recording 135

constructive interference 84, 88, 91

current gain 110, 120

damping 26, 31–3, 34, 37

DC amplifier 113

decibel 112, 120–1

density 57, 75

dependent variable 74, 80

destructive interference 84, 88, 91

diffraction 84, 85–6, 91

digital 126, 127, 132

digital-to-analogue converter 130, 132

discos 135

displacement 21

distortion 129–30

divers 57

ear 24
   eardrum 24
   inner ear 24

eddy vibrations 51

edge tones 51

effective gain 140, 141

electromagnetic induction 96–8, 100, 106, 126

end correction 64–6, 68

energy 9, 42
   elastic potential 26–7

kinetic 23, 27
potential 27
strain 46–7
equalizer 110–11, 121
equilibrium position 26, 37

flat response 114, 121
force
driving 29
friction 26
restoring 29
tension 42, 44–5, 68
forced vibrations 29–31, 37
free vibrations 24–5, 33, 37
frequency 10, 11, 14–16, 21, 37
beat 89, 91
driving 52
fundamental 48, 68
mass per unit length 45–6
natural 24, 26–9
pipes 57–62
resonant 47–8, 54, 58–9, 68
simple harmonic motion 28–9
string tension 44–5
wavelength 16–18
fundamental frequency 48, 68

gain 110, 112, 121
control 111, 121
current 110, 120
effective 140, 141
power 110, 112, 121
voltage 110, 114, 122
gas
adiabatic change 76
isothermal change 76

halls
design 136–40
effective gain 140, 141
pin-drop test 140, 142
reverberation time 139, 140, 142
Symphony Hall, Birmingham 136–8

harmonic 48–50, 60, 68
content 64, 68
headphones 117, 119
hearing threshold 112–13, 121–2
heliox 57
helium 57

induced e.m.f. 98, 106
induction, electromagnetic 96–8, 100, 106, 126
inertia 80
inertial 75
instruments see musical instruments
integrated circuit 114, 121
intensity 14, 21, 140
interference 87–8
constructive 84, 88, 91
destructive 84, 88, 91
iron oxide 125
isothermal 76, 80

Kennedy, Nigel 49, 50
kinetic energy 23, 27
kinetic theory 72, 73, 80

laser 131
lip vibrations 51
longitudinal waves 24, 33, 37
loudness 8, 14–16, 21
see also intensity
loudspeaker 21, 100–5
aperture 85–6
cone 29, 100, 101, 104

magnet 96, 97
magnetic
field 97, 100
flux density 102, 106
force 102–3
magnetic tape 94, 119, 124–6
magnetization 125, 133
mains hum 110
mass per unit length 42, 45–6, 68

microphone 12, 21, 96–100

moving coil microphone 96, 98, 100, 106, 117

musical instruments 41–68

    stringed 42–50

    wind 51–67

musical sounds 12, 21

natural frequency 24, 26–9

Newton, Sir Isaac 76

node 49, 68

noise 12–13, 21, 110

    circuit noise 110

open pipes 52, 68

oscilloscope 12, 13, 21

out of phase 19–20, 84

overblowing 60, 68

overtones 60

pendulums

    Barton's pendulums 30–2

    natural frequency 29

phase 19, 21, 37

    anti-phase 19–20, 84

    difference 19–20, 84

    in phase 19–20, 84, 91

    out of phase 19–20, 84

pin-drop test 140, 142

pipes

    see also air columns

    closed 52, 68

    end correction 64–6

    frequencies 57–62

    open 52, 68

    resonance 63–4

pitch 8, 14–16, 21, 57, 76

playback amplifier 111

potential energy 27

power amplifier 110, 111, 121

power gain 110, 112, 121

pressure 33, 63

    atmospheric 24

    waves 24

quality 49, 64, 68

rarefaction 33, 37, 55, 56, 60

recording amplifier 110–11

reflection 36, 139–40

resolution 130, 133

resonance 37, 47–8, 52, 52–4, 68

resonant frequency 47–8, 54, 57–9, 68

reverberate 139, 143

reverberation time 139, 140, 142

ripple tank 85

sampling 127–9

signal generator 21

simple harmonic motion 28–9, 37

sonometer 42, 43

sound

    beats 89, 91

    diffraction 85–6

    intensity 14, 21, 140

    interference 87–8

    loudest tolerable 112

    pitch 14–16

    quality 49, 64, 68

    recording 94, 96–100, 135

    reproduction 94, 100–5

    stereophonic 117–19

    timbre 49, 64, 68

    transmission 24

    velocity in air 19–20, 56–7, 66–7, 75–8

    velocity in solids 78–9

sound track 135

spring constant 26, 37

springs 23, 26–7

standing waves *see* stationary waves

stationary waves 33, 34–5, 37, 55

stereophonic sound 117–19

strain 46–7

stress 46–7

string
    stationary wave 35
    vibrations 43–4, 46–50
    wave velocity 74–5

stringed instruments 42–50

Symphony Hall, Birmingham 136–8

Tacoma Narrows suspension bridge (USA) 47

tape
    cassette 135
    magnetic 119, 124–6, 194
    video 126

tape-head gap 125, 133

temperature 76–8
    scales 77

tension 42, 44–5, 68

tesla 102

threshold of hearing 112–13, 121–2

timbre 49, 64, 68

tone 51, 111, 122
    edge tone 51

transducers 95, 106
    loudspeakers 21, 100–5
    microphones 12, 21, 96–100

transverse waves 33, 34, 37

travelling waves 33, 34, 35, 37

treble control 110, 111, 122

tuning fork 24, 38, 43, 52

ultrasound 57

velocity
    sound in air 19–20, 56–7, 66–7, 75–8
    sound in solids 78–9
    string waves 74–5

vibrational mode 48, 68

vibration 11, 23
    amplitude 29, 31, 34, 35, 47, 48
    clamped reed 51
    damped 26, 31–4, 37
    eddy 51

    forced 29–31, 37
    free 24–5, 33, 37
    lip 51
    natural frequency 26–9
    period of vibration 30
    string 43–4, 46–50

videotape 126

vinyl discs 135

voltage gain 110, 114, 122

wavelength 11, 14, 16–18, 22

waves
    amplitude 10, 11, 13, 14, 21
    diffraction 84, 85–6, 91
    frequency 11, 14–16
    interference 84, 87–8, 91
    longitudinal 24, 33, 37
    peak 20, 21
    pressure 24
    reflection 36
    standing see waves, stationary
    stationary 33, 34–5, 37, 55
    string 74–5
    transverse 33, 34, 37
    travelling 33, 34, 35, 37
    trough 20, 21
    velocity 16–18, 74–5

wind instruments 51–67

Young modulus 46–7, 78

Young's twin slit experiment 88